Published 2014 by Colourpoint Books
an imprint of Colourpoint Creative Ltd
Colourpoint House, Jubilee Business Park
21 Jubilee Road, Newtownards, BT23 4YH
Tel: 028 9182 6339
Fax: 028 9182 1900
E-mail: info@colourpoint.co.uk
Web: www.colourpoint.co.uk

First Edition
First Impression

Copyright © Colourpoint Books, 2014
Text © Roland Link, 2014
Rare Vinyl Guide © Ian Templeton, 2014
Illustrations © Various, as acknowledged on pages 107 and 120

All rights reserved. No part of this publication may be reproduced, stored in a retrieval system or transmitted in any form or by any means, electronic, mechanical, photocopying, scanning, recording or otherwise, without the prior written permission of the copyright owners and publisher of this book.

The author has asserted his right under the Copyright, Designs and Patents Act, 1988, to be identified as author of this work.

A catalogue record for this book is available from the British Library.

Designed by April Sky Design, Newtownards
Tel: 028 9182 7195
Web: www.aprilsky.co.uk

Printed by GPS Colour Graphics Ltd, Belfast

ISBN 978-1-78073-056-1

Front cover: SLF, February 1980, London © Chris Gabrin
Rear cover: SLF, 2 September 1979 at Brockwell Park, London © Barry Plummer

# What You See Is What You Get...
# STIFF LITTLE FINGERS
## 1977–1983

ROLAND LINK

*Including Rare Vinyl Guide by Ian Templeton*

**COLOURPOINT BOOKS**

Stiff Little Fingers circa 1979
(L to R) Jake Burns, Ali McMordie, Jim Reilly and Henry Cluney.

*"No Stiff Little Fingers, no U2. It's as simple as that."*
*Nicky Tesco (The Members)*

# RIGID DIGITS MUSIC

12 SHARMAN ROAD  BELFAST  BT9 5FW  NORTHERN IRELAND

a registered company

## Contents

| | |
|---|---|
| **Foreword** | 6 |
| **Introduction** | 7 |
| **1977** | 8 |
| **1978** | 10 |
| **1979** | 22 |
| **1980** | 52 |
| **1981** | 76 |
| **1982** | 88 |
| **1983** | 104 |
| **Rare Vinyl Guide** | 108 |

Original Unused Rigid Digits headed paper

What you see is what you get…
STIFF LITTLE FINGERS

## Foreword

In 1978, aged just 15, Jane Williams and I, who were massive Tom Robinson Band fans, went to see TRB band at several UK venues. At the first gig, we were waiting excitedly for the band to come on, not particularly looking forward to the support band, when this group of lads in leather jackets literally exploded onto the stage! It truly was one of those moments where your jaw drops to the floor in awe! They were Stiff Little Fingers – full of energy and anger and passion.

We saw them support TRB at several gigs and totally fell in love with the songs and the music. At home listening to John Peel in the evenings, he was playing SLF's music over and over – we were hooked.

We wanted to know more about this group so we went to London to Rough Trade to ask if this band had a fan club. They didn't at the time, so we volunteered! We also bought copies of the homemade 'Suspect Device' single. Geoff Travis put us in touch with Gordon Ogilvie. Reading the history of the band now, I had no idea we were involved at such an early stage.

We met up with the band and Gordon and set up the fan club in the back room of my mum and dad's house in Park Road, Didcot. I'm sure my parents had thought it would be a five-minute wonder, with a few letters coming through the letterbox. When SLF advertised the fan club on the album covers, we were soon inundated – literally hundreds of letters flooding in. We used to hand write replies to all of them (no PCs in those days!) and send the fans signed pictures and tour dates. We would forward letters on to Gordon for the guys. Fans would send birthday and Christmas cards to them.

**Sarah Woods**
co-founder/president of SLF Fan club 1978-1983

We had our 'regulars', one girl in particular, Vanda, who was an incredible artist – would draw amazing graphics in her letters and on the envelopes. There were also two prisoners who were regular correspondents, although our parents were not too keen on us replying to them, one being captive in the high security prison on the Isle of Wight! He called himself Ginger John and said he could arrange for Jane and I to go to London and meet The Stranglers. My dad put his foot down at this stage!

Every evening and weekend was filled with writing to fans all over the country; this was done in-between our college work! We used to try to get through at least 50 replies each on every session, and made sure people were not kept waiting, particularly for tour dates. The fans were thrilled to receive autographed postcards of the group. We even had fans turning up at the house – two of them came all the way from Scotland.

We went on tour with the band, I'm amazed that our parents consented, but the guys looked after us like little sisters. Tour manager Andi Banks and Gordon always made sure we were in a safe place at the side of the stage. Afterwards in the dressing room, fans would even ask us for our autographs!

When Jane and I turned 18, within a month of each other, we went to London to see the final cut of an album (I think it was 'Nobody's Heroes'). They took us for a meal in the smartest restaurant we'd ever been in (at 18) and they gave Jane a gold bracelet and myself a gold necklace with SLF on – still treasured over 30 years later! Ali and Gordon also came to our house to give us each a Gold Disc of 'Inflammable Material' – again much treasured.

We continued the fan club all the way through college, but got to aged 20 and decided with work commitments that we could not continue. With huge regret we wrote to Gordon to tell him. I didn't know that the band was pretty much coming to the end by then also.

I've met people in work and social circles that I've discovered were into the band all those years ago, including a life long friend who swears he wrote to the fan club and didn't get a reply – I swear he did!

We had the most fantastic time!

## Introduction

The idea for *What You See Is What You Get…* initially came about during the writing of *Kicking Up A Racket – The Story of Stiff Little Fingers 1977–1983*. During the research for that book I turned up a number of posters, badges, tickets, reviews, interviews and, probably of most interest to Stiff Little Fingers' fans, unpublished photographs.

Some of the photographs and newspaper clippings included herein are of fairly dubious quality and I'm absolutely sure that others would never have got past a professional photographer's original edit. However, as my primary motivation for putting *What You See Is What You Get…* together was to share with other SLF fans some rarer images of the band, supported by a smattering of memorabilia from the time period, I've included them all the same.

I've also included a fair number of photographs that were used at the time for promotional purposes, a decision I arrived at primarily because I feel that these 'classic' Stiff Little Fingers images belong in a book of this nature: they were chosen first time around for a reason!

Although I've covered the band's original career, images from the very beginning and very end of this time period are notoriously few and far between. During all my time researching the group I've only ever turned up two shots credited as taken in 1977; both in November of that year. Although the one which originally appeared in 1981's 'Go For It' UK tour program was almost certainly taken in early 1978. Both are included here. From 1983 just four photographs have surfaced, three of which I used in *Kicking Up A Racket* the fourth is unusable. Sarah Woods, who along with Jane Williams, ran SLF's fan club from 1978–1983, clearly remembers taking photos of the band at the two farewell shows in February 1983, but alas they seem to have disappeared into the mists of time (or more probably Sarah thinks the dustbin).

Therefore, as far as I know, and I'd love to be proved wrong on this, no photo sessions or live shots exist of the band from these years. Hardly surprising as the group played just five shows in 1977 and two farewell dates in 1983. As a consequence I've had to turn to printed articles to cover these sections of the book.

Of course a project such as this can never hope to include every piece of SLF memorabilia or photograph from the time frame and indeed, neither does it set out to do so. I've deliberately avoided including the large amount of music paper interviews, printed news items, record company circulars, adverts for shows and releases and the inevitable plethora of 'titbit' news items that appeared over the course of the six years covered. I've also had to be very strict with myself while examining contact sheets, particular photo sessions and live shots; and have had to admit defeat (very reluctantly) with concern to securing the use of some other fantastic images that I know exist. You can't win them all however hard you try!

All the best,
**Roland Link**

This book would not have been possible without the help, encouragement and support of many people.

My sincerest thanks go to the managers and band members from the time period – Brian Faloon; Ali McMordie; Jake Burns; Henry Cluney; Jim Reilly; Dolphin Taylor; Gordon Ogilvie; and Colin McClelland.

I'm also much indebted to the photographers whose images appear within these pages.

The following individuals contributed in many different ways, each very much appreciated – Wayne Connolly; Andy 'Biggs' Graham; Terri Hooley; Daphne Link; Sean O'Neill; 'Big' Dennis Pinnock; Ian Templeton; Dave Tulacz; Mick Warrender; and Len and Sarah Woods.

Colourpoint's Malcolm Johnston has my heartfelt gratitude; firstly for believing in the project enough to publish *What You See Is What You Get…* and secondly for the inordinate amount of hours spent in consultation concerning design and re-design of the book.

Special thanks go to my wife Anna who, as always, supported and encouraged me all the way.

# 1977
nineteen seventy seven

Named after a Vibrators' track, Belfast's Stiff Little Fingers formed in the summer of 1977. Up until that point school friends Jake Burns (lead vocals/guitar), Henry Cluney (rhythm guitar/backing vocals and occasional lead vocals) and Brian Faloon (drums) had spent the previous couple of years playing heavy rock covers as Highway Star. With Henry's discovery of all things punk, starting with the Sex Pistols' 'Anarchy In The UK', Jake's new found love for Graham Parker and Elvis Costello, and a mutual appreciation of Eddie And The Hotrods and the nascent Clash, the writing was on the wall for Highway Star.

With the addition of bassist Ali McMordie, a set of punk cover versions and one original song was worked up. The group debuted live on 16 August 1977, incidentally the same night Elvis Presley died. By the end of the year the band had played five local shows. It was at the fourth of these, staged at the ramshackle Glenmachan Stables on 14 November, that journalists Gordon Ogilvie and Colin McClelland caught the band's performance. Instantly hooked they agreed to manage the band.

*Left:* Henry Cluney, Ali McMordie, Jake Burns and Brian Faloon. The earliest known photograph of Stiff Little Fingers. The image originally appeared in Alwyn Greer's *Private World* fanzine in November 1977.

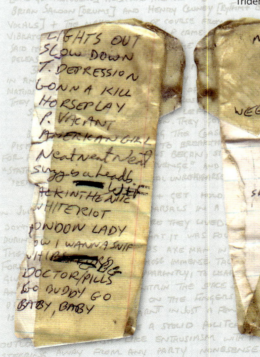

An original ticket for the band's one and only appearance at the Trident in Bangor.

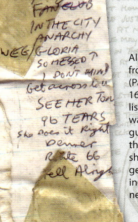

Ali McMordie's original set list from the band's debut show at (Paddy) Lambes Lounge, Belfast, 16 August 1977. The 33 song set list, which measures 1 x 6 inches, was originally taped to his bass guitar. Ali: "When I rediscovered this set list 35 years later and showed it to Jake he was genuinely shocked at the songs included on it. He still swears he's never played some of them!"

From the band's formation in the summer of 1977, Jake attempted to garner publicity for the group by periodically writing to *Belfast Sunday News* journalist Colin McClelland.

*Right:* Colin's review of the band's first Glenmachan Stables show, 14 November 1977, which appeared in his *Belfast Sunday News* 'Follow Me Around' column, 20 November 1977.

Directly after the show Colin and fellow journalist Gordon Ogilvie became the band's co-managers.

---

I HAVE received several letters from a strange group of people who call themselves Stiff Little Fingers.

To get them off my back, I have decided to publish the last of their missives in full. And as this has been a very boring column so far, you will obviously not mind being bored just a little more.

"We now feel the world is ready to know about us through your wonderfully informative pages. We, in case you haven't already guessed, are Stiff Little Fingers. We are also far, far, better than Candy (who used to be a pop group anyway! Stacks of credibility). I'll give you a run - down on the band personnel:

"Brian Faloon — drums and concussion; Alistair Jardine McMordie — bass extraordinaire; Jake — guitar and vocals; Albert Clock — guitar and vocals.

"Not only are we a spiffy cover version band but we write some extremely jolly ditties.

"We are looking for lots of lovely work that will bring us lots of lovely money so we can afford to pay for real advertisements and not have to resort to cheap gimmicks like this to get space in a truly wonderful publication as yours. (Stop crawling!).

"So, I hope this load of nonsense is of some use to you. At least it shows we do exist and we are not either a Jim Armstrong Band nor are we boring.

"Peace and Love, Jake (a stiff little finger).

"PS. Anyone who wants to give us the above - mentioned 'lovely work' should ring Belfast 770969 for details (ask for Henry)."

How absolutely fascinating, Jake. If you are as boring on stage as you are on paper, you'll probably make the top.

*Above:* The first piece about the band that Colin wrote for the *Belfast Sunday News*. It appeared in his weekly 'Follow Me Around' column, 21 August 1977.

*Note:* 'Albert Clock' was Henry, who briefly named himself after the Belfast city centre time piece.

---

Stiff Little Fingers, that aggressive new Belfast punk outfit, would like you all to know that they'll be supporting the Damned at Queen's University on November 16

New Wave supporters probably already know about the Belfast dates of Clash (October 20), and the Stranglers (November 8), but Stiff Little Fingers would also like to point out that they play an independent gig with the Heavy Water Blues Band on November 14 at Glenmachan Tower Hotel, and that tickets for this event (only 60p) will shortly be available from Rocky Mungo's Record Pit in Linenhall Street in the near future.

---

# Punk rock around the clock

Ogilvie invites me to Glenmachan Tower Hotel, where there is a punk/blues party in the Stables.

If you are ever thinking of visiting a punk/blues party I should perhaps advise you not to wear your best suit, or dress.

Punks go in a lot for good-natured spitting and jumping around, bumping into people. You might have your drink accidentally spilled over you, or get wet the other way.

Actually, punks seem to have a pretty good time when they're out to enjoy themselves.

The punk dance is called the pogo, which consists of jumping up and down on one spot for a long time. This sometimes tires the punks out so much that they fall down. It is not unusual to see a large pile of wriggling punks on the floor at the end of a dance.

Punk males dress in either 1950-style suits with schoolboy ties, or in torn denims with the obligatory safety pins holding the whole thing together. Some wear big boots.

There are not many female punks at the Stables, but there are a couple of young ladies in torn T-shirts. This is rather disappointing, as I was hoping to meet the girl I'd seen in the Europa Hotel last month who was wearing a spiked red dog collar and a blue laundary bag.

Some of the punks I spoke to at the Stables were very annoyed about the way three recent rock shows they'd wanted to see at the Ulster Hall had been cancelled because of insurance.

I agreed with them.

Bryan Young, who plays with the local group Rudi, said that it was very hard for home-grown punk bands to get places here to play. The venue might be booked, but almost certainly the hotel or club owner will get to hear the dreaded word 'punk' and cancel the booking.

Bryan's band plays at the Trident in Bangor some weeks.

The reason for our visit to the Stables was not only to make contact with the punks, but also to hear the band Stiff Little Fingers, who have been writing to me for months now, telling me how good they were.

I was surprised to find that they were right.

Stiff Little Fingers are a very good band indeed, by anybody's reckoning. I think you'll be hearing more of them in the near future.

Anyway, that was our Punk Night Out. I think that punks are probably a much maligned group of people. A little outrageous in their dress, a bit aggressive now and again, but then look what people used to say about Beatles fans.

I think we're going to have to learn to live with punk rock. I don't think it will just go away. It might take a bit of time to get used to the spitting, though.

# 1978
nineteen seventy eight

*I'm a suspect device*

*Above:* (L to R) Henry, Brian, Jake and Ali at one of the turn-style gates in the 'ring of steel' barricade, which surrounded Belfast's city centre, summer 1978.

Upon becoming Stiff Little Fingers' co-manager, Gordon Ogilvie agreed to finance the release of the band's debut single. Recorded in early February and released on St Patrick's Day (17 March), on the band's own Rigid Digits label, 'Suspect Device' (Jake and Gordon's first collaboration) b/w Jake's 'Wasted Life' was the group's opening salvo. Picked up by hugely influential BBC Radio One DJ John Peel and given repeated spins, the band suddenly found themselves almost unable to keep up with demand. After the original 500 discs quickly sold out several re-presses had to be ordered.

Interest from Island Records saw the band record demos for the company in May. The results led to a 'word of mouth' agreement that Stiff Little Fingers could consider themselves Island Records' recording artists. It wasn't to be however, as upon returning from a business trip to Jamaica the label's head honcho, Chris Blackwell, vetoed the deal.

Peaceline pose between the Shankill and Falls, Belfast.

At this point Geoff Travis, owner of independent London record shop and recently formed record label, Rough Trade, stepped in. Having already helped distribute the band's debut single, Geoff offered to release their second. Rather than go to the expense of re-recording material, the Island demo session tapes were 'secured'. Differing accounts exist as to how this was done, depending on who you ask! Producer Doug Bennett was employed to remix the tracks.

'Alternative Ulster' b/w "78 RPM' was released in October; by which time the band were on a UK tour supporting the Tom Robinson Band. Jake had originally written to TRB asking if SLF could have the opening slot. The answer had been no, but when original tour support, Third World, dropped out at the last minute Tom was mighty keen to employ the young, brash, explosive Belfast band's services.

With 'Alternative Ulster' riding high in the independent charts, fast-spreading rave word-of-mouth live performance reviews and their first music weekly front cover courtesy of *Sounds*, things should have been on the up and up for the combo. In reality nothing was further from the truth. Gordon and Colin hadn't received a single enquiry or offer from any record company. Even worse, Brian Faloon was determined to stick to his decision, announced just prior to the TRB support dates, that he was going to quit the band.

During a backstage chat with Jake and Gordon at one of the TRB tour's London shows, Geoff Travis confirmed he would be happy to release the band's debut LP. It would be Rough Trade's first long player after a series of 7"s. As for Brian, he had no problem hanging around long enough to play on the album. Produced by Geoff Travis and Red Crayola's Mayo Thompson at Cambridge's Spaceward Studios during a couple of weeks in November, 'Inflammable Material' stands as an undisputed classic slice of explosive, taut, tuneful punk rock. With the recording completed Brian headed home to Belfast. After a fairly fraught couple of weeks auditioning hopefuls, the band had received a phone call from one Jim Reilly announcing he was their new drummer. He wasn't wrong! Although also a Belfast native, at the time of his successful audition Jim was living in Sheffield cleaning windows for a living. Once he'd relocated to London the band ended the year with a short Christmas tour of Ireland.

The front cover of *Laughing Gravy* fanzine. The photograph, taken in Northumberland Street, Belfast (between the Falls and Shankill Roads), came from the same session that provided the shot which appeared on the back cover of the band's debut single.

*Above:* (L to R) Jake, Ali, Henry and Brian. Stiff Little Fingers at a rehearsal in St Peter's Church of Ireland Hall, Antrim Road, North Belfast.

The photo was eventually included in the band's 1981 'Go For It' UK tour program, where it was credited as being taken in November 1977. It is more likely, however, that it originates from early 1978.

*Left and below:* March 1978 'Suspect Device'/'Wasted Life' demo tape front cover. Twelve copies were produced and sent to record companies and radio stations.

An original poster for the band's eighth show.

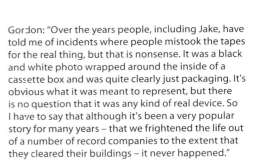

Gordon: "Over the years people, including Jake, have told me of incidents where people mistook the tapes for the real thing, but that is nonsense. It was a black and white photo wrapped around the inside of a cassette box and was quite clearly just packaging. It's obvious what it was meant to represent, but there is no question that it was any kind of real device. So I have to say that although it's been a very popular story for many years – that we frightened the life out of a number of record companies to the extent that they cleared their buildings – it never happened."

*Right:* An original ticket from the band's Glenmachan Stables show. The gig was organised primarily to introduce the group to a number of 'movers and shakers' in the media field.

*Right:* An advert from the 'End Of The World' Southern and Northern Irish Tour, 10–22 April 1978, with Blue Steam and Cobra (later replaced by Curse). From 'Swingscene' *Belfast Sunday News*, 9 April 1978.

□ BELOW: Rock stars relaxing with their ladies (from left) Jake, Jackie, Brian, Barbara, Ali and Fiona. Wonder who bought them all that drink? Thanks for playing, lads.

□ And where's Henry, come to think of it?

*Above: Hot Press* report on SLF falling foul of a no new wave bands ban by Dublin's Baggot Inn, during the 'End Of The World' tour.

Photograph taken in the Duke of York public house, Commercial Court, Belfast, January 1978

Colin ensured the Stables' show received publicity. This piece featured in his 'Follow Me Around' column in the *Belfast Sunday News*, 2 April 1978.

13

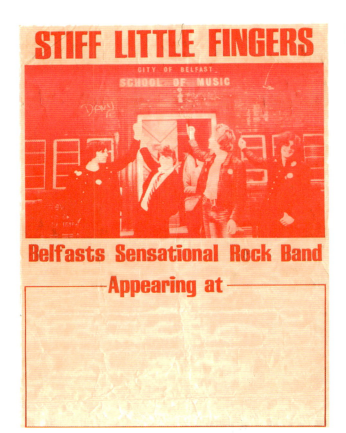
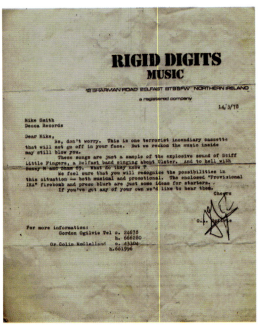

*Above:* Rigid Digits letter to Decca Records.
*Left:* 1978 Generic 'Belfast' Poster.

*All photos:* Harp Bar, Belfast, 7 July 1978.
This was the band's second of three appearances at the legendary venue.

Tom Robinson Band's 'Power In the Darkness' UK Tour 1 September–21 October 1978.
Stiff Little Fingers supported at all shows.

Stiff Little Fingers in front of Tom Robinson Band's drum kit. City Hall, Newcastle-Upon-Tyne, 27 September 1978.

*Above and left:* Ali and Jake, City Hall, Newcastle-Upon-Tyne, 27 September 1978.

**CITY HALL**
Northumberland Road, Newcastle upon Tyne 1

Wednesday, 27th September, 1978, at 7.30 p.m.

OUTLAW CONCERTS
present

**Tom Robinson Band
in concert
plus Third World Band**

AREA £2.20   SEAT   E 24

Booking Agents: City Hall Box Office
Northumberland Road, Newcastle upon Tyne (Tel. 20007)
*This Portion to be retained.*

SMITH PRINT GROUP

A ticket from the show, still showing original support band Third World.

Brian, City Hall, Newcastle-Upon-Tyne, 27 September 1978. The TRB support slot would be the only UK tour that Brian would undertake with the band.

*All photos:* Backstage, City Hall, Newcastle-Upon-Tyne, 27 September 1978.

'78 RPM badge was given away on the tour.

SLF with a Geordie fan named Brian, who over the next couple of years attended a number of the band's Northern English shows.

*Right:* Whitla Hall, Queen's University, Belfast, 15 October 1978. Henry: "We came home to a hero's welcome. We couldn't believe it!"

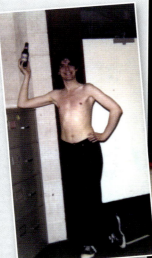

*Above:* Jake on the TRB tour September/October 1978.

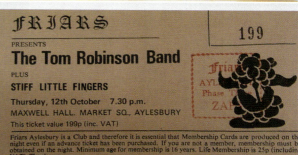

Brian Faloon, Venue unknown.

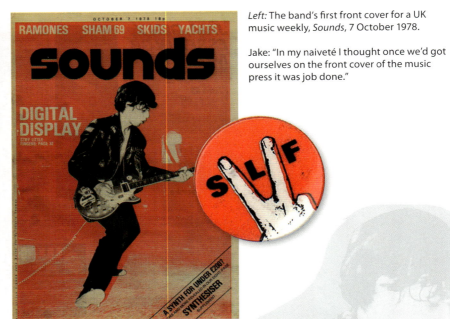

*Left:* The band's first front cover for a UK music weekly, *Sounds*, 7 October 1978.

Jake: "In my naiveté I thought once we'd got ourselves on the front cover of the music press it was job done."

New University of Ulster, Coleraine, 16 October 1978.

Warwick University, Coventry, 18 October 1978.

*All photos:* taken during the TRB's 'Power In The Darkness' UK tour.

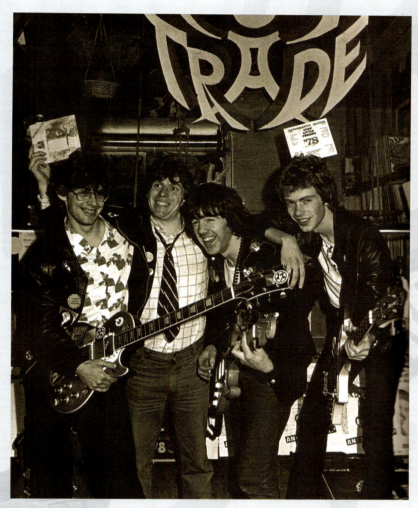

The band members celebrate the release of 'Alternative Ulster' outside the Rough Trade shop, Notting Hill, London, October 1978.

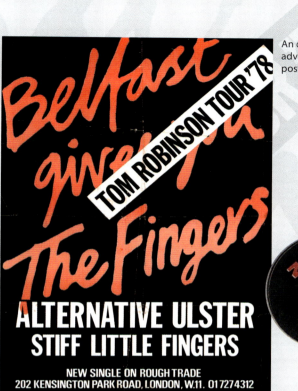

An original advertisement poster for the single.

*Right:* Colin McClelland's personal copy of the single, on which he scribbled an initial list of the band's Christmas 1978 Irish tour dates.

# 1979
nineteen seventy nine

The band began the year with back-to-back home town shows at the Pound Music Club. It was to be the last club dates they'd play in the city. Released at the start of February, 'Inflammable Material' tied in with the 'Rough Trade' UK package tour, Stiff Little Fingers' first headline jaunt around mainland Britain. Picking up rave reviews for both album and shows the band was suddenly big news. Significantly 'Inflammable Material' became the first totally independent album to scale the UK Album Charts' Top 20 and the band's popularity rocketed. The record peaked at No 14, with rumours circulating at the time that it would have crashed the Top 10 if it hadn't been held back by the 'powers that be'. The 'Rough Trade' club dates were inundated by hundreds of enthusiastic fans and numerous journalists from the UK's big three music weeklies were dispatched to cover events. It was also at this juncture that a large number of the major record labels finally woke-up to the band. After a Rough Trade re-release of 'Suspect Device' b/w 'Wasted Life' a year to the day that it originally came out, one final single, 'Gotta Gettaway' b/w 'Bloody Sunday' was released through Rough Trade in May. The 'Gotta Gettaway' UK tour, the band's first headline tour in theatre sized venues, supported the release.

Over the summer Stiff Little Fingers also played a couple of festivals in Sweden and Finland, their first shows outside the UK and Southern Ireland. In August the band signed with Chrysalis Records. The first release for the label was September's 'Straw Dogs' b/w 'You Can't Say Crap On The Radio'. With major label support and yet another trek around the UK on the 'Guts For Sale' tour, the single proved to be the band's first 7" to bother the national UK charts at No 44.

The end of the year was spent in the studio recording the second LP, 'Nobody's Heroes', for the sessions the band again employed the services of Doug Bennett.

Stiff Little Fingers downtown Belfast, January 1979.

*All photos:* The Pound Music Club, Belfast, 9 and 10 January 1979.

*All photos:* The Pound Music Club, Belfast, 9 and 10 January 1979. These shows proved to be the last times that the band would play at the venue, or any other pub or club sized venues in their home town.

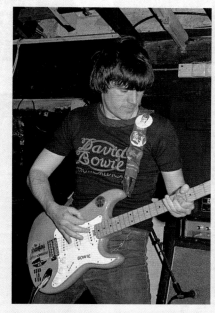

What you see is what you get...
STIFF LITTLE FINGERS

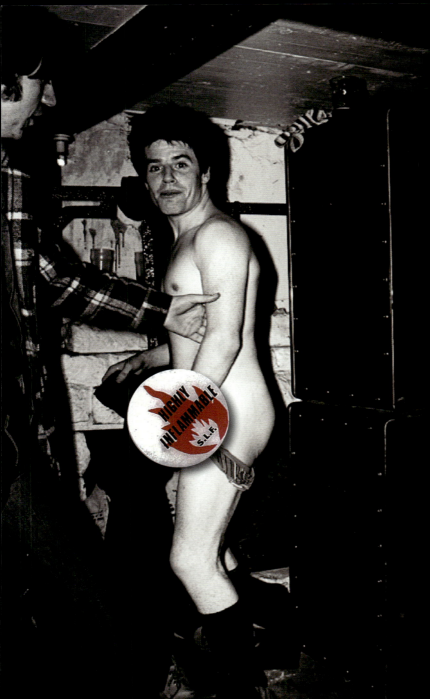

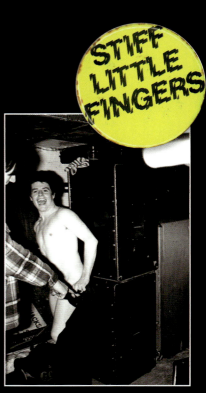

The Pound Music Club, Belfast,
9 and 10 January 1979.

*Left:* The new Stiff Little Fingers line up rock the Pound Music Club, Belfast, January 1979. (L to R) Jim, Henry, Ali and Jake.

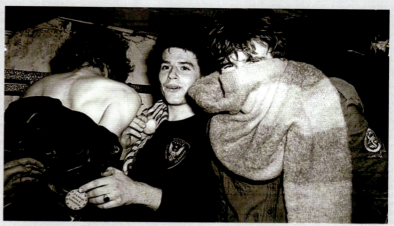

Jake, Jim and Henry getting changed at the Pound Music Club.

Downtown Belfast in the snow, January 1979. (L to R) Jake, Ali and Henry.

Photographer Sean Hennessey: "SLF walking home from the gig at the Pound in the snow; no tour bus/limo for them, or the photographer. A six mile walk for most of us."

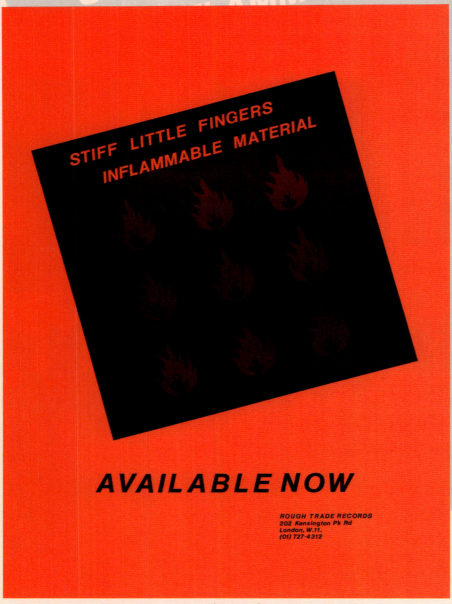

The late Seventies, Camden, London based fanzine *In The City* (#9).

An original Rough Trade promotional card.

An original Rough Trade advertisement poster for the 'Inflammable Material' album. Another version of the poster showed the reverse of the LP sleeve.

'Rough Trade' UK Tour 2 February–10 March 1979. **Support acts:** Essential Logic and Robert Rental & The Normal.

Original 'Rough Trade' UK tour poster, plus tickets and a pass.

*All photos:* 'Rough Trade' UK tour, Friars, Aylesbury, 3 February 1979.

An original flyer for the show.

'Rough Trade' UK tour, Stowaway Club, Newport, 14 February 1979.

Henry: "I remember that leather jacket that Jake wore on the 'Rough Trade' tour, from about halfway through the dates he could take it off after the shows and stand it on a table or wherever and it'd stand up on its own. It was completely rigid with sweat."

Stowaway Club, Newport, 14 February 1979.

The glamour of the rock 'n' roll lifestyle. Sharing a pot of tea.

*All photos:* A bed and breakfast establishment in Newport, February 1979.

Jim discusses the finer points of the 'Inflammable Material' LP with a female fan. Jim: "Yeah, I had a lot of fun in that band!"

Jake and Jim *(top left)* and Ali *(top right)* at the Drill Hall, Lincoln, 1 March 1979.

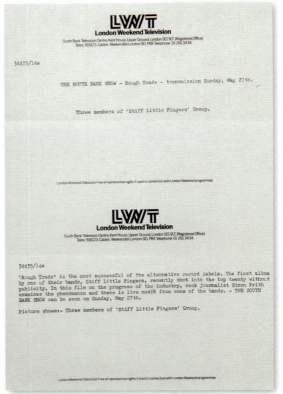

*Right and above:* London Weekend Television *South Bank Show* correspondence plus accompanying photograph, taken during the 'Rough Trade' tour dates.

An original poster for a standalone show, March 1979 at the Lyceum.

A set of original promotional cards.

*Above:* Original summer 1979 promotional card. The photo was taken in a children's playground just behind the Rough Trade shop.

Part of Rock Against Racism's 'Militant Entertainment' UK Tour 27–30 March 1979.

*All photos:* Clouds, Edinburgh, 27 March 1979.

**'Gotta Gettaway' UK Tour 19 May–10 June 1979. Support act:** The Starjets.

*Both photos:* 14 April 1979, final night of Rock Against Racism's 'Militant Entertainment' UK tour, Alexander Palace, London (the track being jammed on was Bob Marley's 'Big Tree, Small Axe').

Jake on stage with (L to R) TRB's guitarist Danny Kustow, Tom Robinson and Generation X's bass player Tony James. Note: This was not an SLF show, Jake made a guest appearance. Others who played on the night included The Ruts, Leyton Buzzards, Aswad, Angelic Upstarts, John Cooper-Clarke, Dambala, Belt And Braces; with guest appearances from Alex Harvey and Sham 69's Jimmy Pursey.

Original advertisement poster for the single, plus a sticker and tour tickets. Jake: "At the time we told people the young boy on the 'Gotta Getaway' single and promotional material was Ali as a wee lad!"

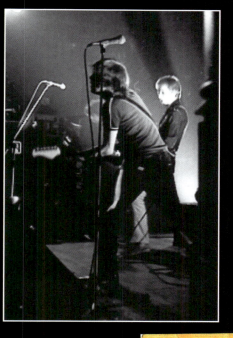

*Both photos:* Ulster Hall, Belfast, 21 May 1979

Jim Reilly, Dread at the controls!

*All photos*: Kingsway Studio, London, during the 'Straw Dogs' single session, 14 August 1979.

*Above:* Finland, 21 or 22 July 1979.

*Left (all photos)*: Pavilion, Hemel Hempstead, 27 May 1979. Against their diamond of fire backdrop the 'Gotta Gettaway' UK tour was the band's first headline outing in UK theatre sized venues.

Carnival Against Racism, Brockwell Park, Brixton, 2 September 1979. Within minutes of these photographs being taken the stage was invaded by members of the audience, the organisers cut the power and the show was abandoned.

Henry: "That started out as a great gig, but in the end so many people got on stage that we had to leave. Gordon got punched by someone during the chaos and I think the stage eventually collapsed."

Individual photographs of the band taken at the show were used on the inlay sleeve of the UK version of the 'Nobody's Heroes' album.
Jim: "I look like I'm trying to catch flies!"

*All photos:* Camden, North West London, summer 1979.

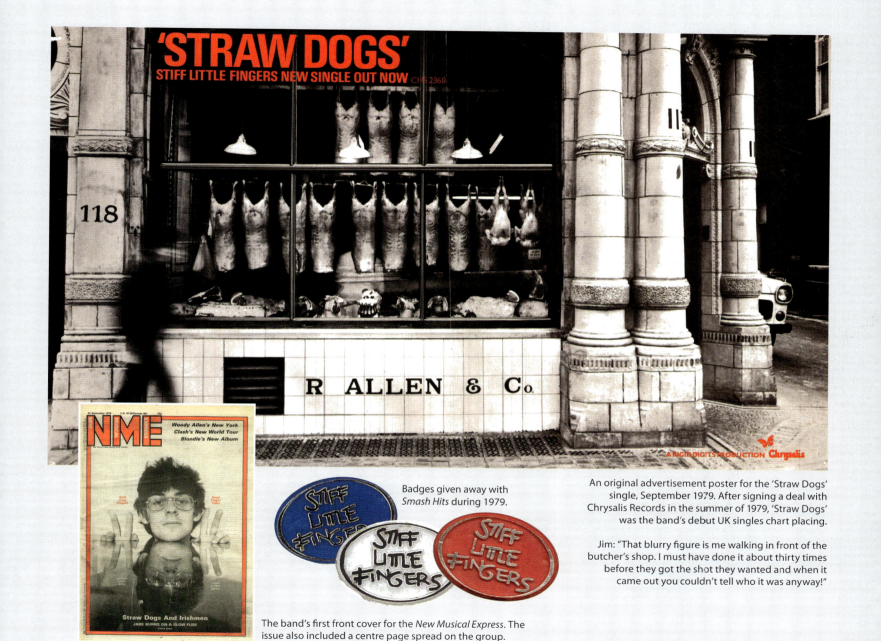

Badges given away with *Smash Hits* during 1979.

The band's first front cover for the *New Musical Express*. The issue also included a centre page spread on the group.

An original advertisement poster for the 'Straw Dogs' single, September 1979. After signing a deal with Chrysalis Records in the summer of 1979, 'Straw Dogs' was the band's debut UK singles chart placing.

Jim: "That blurry figure is me walking in front of the butcher's shop. I must have done it about thirty times before they got the shot they wanted and when it came out you couldn't tell who it was anyway!"

*All photos:* Camden, North West London, summer 1979.

**'Guts For Sale' UK Tour 5–23 October 1979. Support act:** The Donkeys.

*This page:* Original 'Guts For Sale' UK tour poster, tickets, Midland Concert Promotions' Access All Areas tour pass and tour badge.

48 What you see is what you get…
STIFF LITTLE FINGERS

*All photos*: 'Guts For Sale' UK tour, Locarno, Bristol, 7 October 1979.

Jake at the Locarno, Bristol, 7 October 1979.

Jim and Ali meet the fans.

hangs out with a David Bowie lookalike.

Ali and Jim backstage, venue unknown.
Jim: "My only excuse for that shirt is that I used to swap with fans if they asked!"

*Above:* An original ticket for the Le Palace, Paris, France show, 16 December 1979.

*Left:* An original poster for the same show. The gig was cancelled and rescheduled for the 13 January 1980. It marked the band's French live debut.

# 1980
### nineteen eighty

SLF began 1980 with a standalone show in Paris, rescheduled from the previous December. In February the lead single from the 'Nobody's Heroes' LP, 'At The Edge' b/w 'Running Bear' and 'White Christmas' (the live silly encores) was released. Building on the chart success of the previous 7" the group found themselves on the BBC's *Top of the Pops* and at No 15 in the UK singles' chart.

Kicking off March with the 26 date 'Nobody's Heroes' UK tour and LP release, a sold out Hammersmith Odeon, acres of column inches, full page interviews in the music press and a No 8 album chart placing confirmed the band's now huge popularity.

The double A-side single 'Tin Soldiers' and 'Nobody's Hero' followed in May and once again the group graced *Top of the Pops*. Possibly because both tracks were already available on the LP the single stalled at No 36.

July's double A-side single, the less abrasive, rockier 'Back To Front' and a pop over-toned cover of the Wailing Souls' 'Mr Fire Coalman', did even less damage to the charts, peaking at No 49. Unfortunately this proved to be the rule rather than the exception for the majority of the band's remaining single releases.

Jake on the cover of *Hot Press*, Dublin's bi-weekly music paper, January 1980.

*All photos*: Lots Road, Chelsea, London, early 1980.

A promotional card from the session.

July also witnessed a short jaunt around Britain. Dubbed the 'School Holidays' tour the dates were primarily undertaken to capture material for a live album. September duly saw its release. Titled 'Hanx!' the tracks recorded at London's Finsbury Park Rainbow (apart from 'Johnny Was', which was culled from the Aylesbury Friars date) captured the band in fine form. Although not completely sold on the idea of releasing a live LP that early in their career – it was primarily undertaken at the behest of Chrysalis as a vehicle with which to introduce the band to the North American market – it did brisk business with the UK fans, reaching No 9. The band hit the USA in October, debuting at Trax nightclub in New York City. They finished out the year with a short round of German dates in November/December.

Town Hall, Guildford, late February 1980.

Freelance photographer Barry Plummer: "I don't really remember too much about this session. I set it up, the guys turned up, we shot it and Chrysalis bought four colour shots from me. That's about it!"

London, February 1980.

*Right:* An original music shop advertisement poster for the 'At The Edge' single, February 1980.

*Below:* An original 1980 poster produced by Scottish company Pace Minerva and sold in Woolworths and WH Smith. The shot was captured during the band's performance of 'At The Edge' on the BBC TV's *Top of the Pops* stage set.

London, February 1980. Shots from this session were used on various promotional materials for the 'Nobody's Heroes' UK tour, US and European dates and a number of magazine interview features.

Shepperton Studios, Shepperton, Surrey, February 1980. The band was using the facility to rehearse for their March 1980 'Nobody's Heroes' UK tour.

*Right:* Town Hall, Guildford, late February 1980.

Henry: "I remember the session well. The photographer tried to get us to strike lots of cheesy poses. We soon told him that we weren't the Bay City Rollers, or whoever. I notice Jim ended up with a chair, typical!"

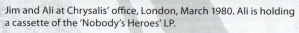

Jim and Ali at Chrysalis' office, London, March 1980. Ali is holding a cassette of the 'Nobody's Heroes' LP.

**'Nobody's Heroes' UK Tour 4–30 March 1980.** *Support act:* Another Pretty Face.

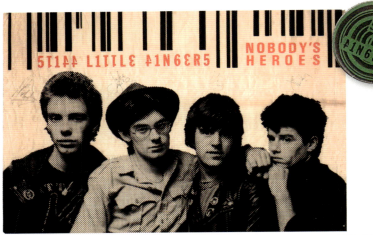

Above: Original 'Nobody's Heroes' tour poster.

Tour posters and passes.

The band and Gordon Ogilvie backstage pre-show at the Sports Centre, Bracknell, 8 March 1980.

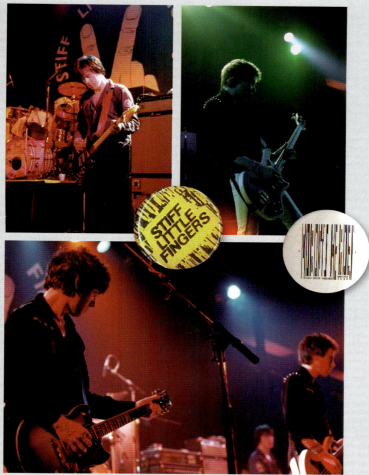

'Nobody's Heroes' UK tour, Sports Centre, Bracknell, 8 March 1980.

Original 'Nobody's Heroes' UK tour tickets.

*Above:* (L to R) Jim Reilly, Andi Banks (tour manager), Jake Burns, Henry Cluney, Ali McMordie, Wally Grove (head of security) and the 'Nobody's Heroes' tour driver in front of the tour bus outside the Stateside Centre, Bournemouth, 9 March 1980.

*Above:* Both photos 'Nobody's Heroes' UK tour, Pavilion, Hemel Hempstead, 20 March 1980.

Two original tickets from the 'Nobody's Heroes' Hammersmith Odeon, London date.

Jake and Jim 'Nobody's Heroes' UK tour, Hammersmith Odeon, London, 23 March 1980.

'Nobody's Heroes' tour, Odeon, Edinburgh, 28 March 1980. Another quiet night!

*Right:* Whiling away the hours on the tour bus playing Headache during the 'Nobody's Heroes' UK tour. (L to R) Unknown, Mel O'Brien, Thomas 'Kidso' Reilly, Siobhan Fahey, Jim Reilly and Pete Barrett.*

Picture of Jake and the one below of Ali and Jim were both taken backstage at the Colston Hall, Bristol, 10 March 1980.

*Left:* A house party at Siobhan Fahey's sister Ann's East London flat. Back row (L to R), Spud Murphy (SLF's back line technician), Anne Stewart, Pete Barrett, Karl Badger, Niamh Fahey, Unknown, Andy Luckett, Vaughn Toulouse (Department S singer), Ali McMordie, Isabelle (Ali's French girlfriend of the time). Front row (L to R) Maire Fahey, Jim Reilly, Siobhan Fahey.

* Pete Barrett along with his partner Nik Egan ran Fly By Night, the company that designed SLF's 'At The Edge' single sleeve.

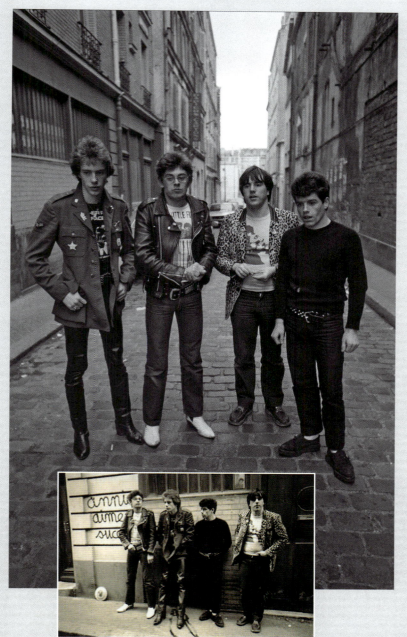

*Top right:* An original poster for the Paradiso, Amsterdam date of the 'Nobody's Heroes' European tour.

*All photos:* Paris, April 1980.

The teen pop approach. The back cover of *My Guy* magazine, June 1980. Taken from the Lots Road, Chelsea photo session it incorrectly identifies Jake as Ali.

The DIY/punk rock approach to magazine production. The front cover of the *Breakout* fanzine. Produced by the people that wrote the *No More Masterpieces* fanzine, it was the only fanzine printed during the band's original career that was dedicated solely to them.

'Schools Holidays' UK Tour 18–29 July 1980. *Support act:* Weapon of Peace.

Various tour posters.

*Left:* An original music shop advertisement poster for the 'Back To Front'/'Mr. Fire Coal Man' single, July 1980.

*All photos:* Backstage on the first night of the 'School Holidays' UK tour at the Winter Gardens, Malvern, 18 July 1980. The same day as the tour started the double A-side single 'Back To Front'/'Mr. Fire Coal Man' was released.

NOBODYS
BARB WIRE
WAIT & SEE
GOT GETAWAY
JOHNNY WAS
BACK TO FRONT
FLY THE FLAG
MAKE IT ALRIGHT
NO CHANGE
ALT ULST
FIRE COALMAN
AT THE EDGE
WASTED LIFE
TIN SOLDIERS

*Left:* 'School Holidays' UK tour set list.

An original promotional card.

*All photos:* Rainbow Theatre, London, 20 July 1980.

The show was recorded and apart from 'Johnny Was', which was culled from the Friars, Aylesbury show five days later, released as the live album 'Hanx!'.

Original Access All Areas passes for the 'School Holidays' Rainbow Theatre, London show.

In a case of recycling, some passes from the previous 'Nobody's Heroes' UK tour were used on the dates.

*Top and bottom left:* Rainbow Theatre, London, 20 July 1980.

*Left:* (L to R) Henry, the UK Subs' Charlie Harper, Jim, American groupie Anna(rexia) Nervosa, Motorhead's Lemmy and John Shiels.

*Left and above:* Friars, Aylesbury, 25 July 1980.

*Both photos:* Friars, Aylesbury, 25 July 1980.
Two backstage passes and tickets from the 'School Holidays' UK tour.

*All photos:* 'Hanx!' album photo session.

Henry: "I'm not absolutely sure, but I'd imagine the shots would have been taken possibly during a sound check."

*Right:* An original 'Hanx!' album advertisement poster, September 1980.

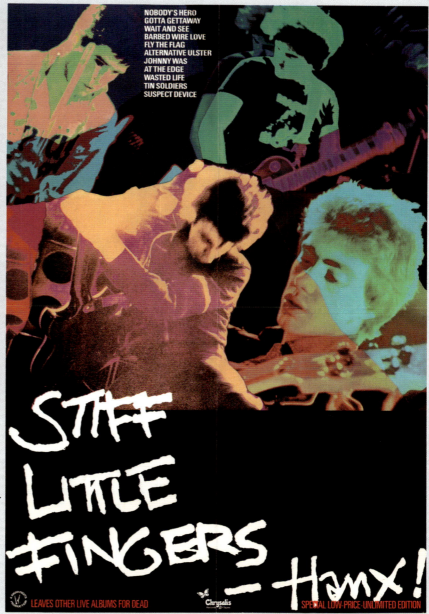

*Left:* Ali. *Right:* Andi Banks (SLF's Tour Manager), Jake and Jim. Both live shots at Trax, New York City, 17 October 1980 (the band's US debut).

*Above:* Jake, Jim and Henry outside New York bar Molly Malones.

Henry, San Francisco Bay on route to Alcatraz.

Gordon and Henry with a San Francisco street car.

*All photos:* Live and backstage, The Keystone, Palo Alto, California, 23 October 1980. With bad acoustics and violent elements within the crowd, the show proved to be one of the lower points on the tour.

Ali: "When Henry's not looking at the camera it's because he'd found out that, apparently, Neil Young never did and he's copying him."

# 1981
nineteen eighty one

January found Stiff Little Fingers back in Belfast performing two ram-packed shows. Filmed for the BBC Northern Ireland's *Stiff Little Finger Play At Home* documentary, the footage captured the band on the cusp of their transition from punk rock band to hard guitar pop act.

February and the first few days in March was spent recording their third studio LP, the melting pot of musical styles – reggae, rockabilly, guitar pop, rock – further confirmed their musical metamorphosis. The record would prove to be the band's most mature and accomplished outing to date. It remains Jake Burn's favourite LP from the band's initial time together.

The following month 'Just Fade Away' b/w the instrumental 'Go For It' and a live version of 'Doesn't Make It Alright' (recorded on the previous year's 'School Holidays' tour) was released. The accompanying *Top of the Pops* appearance found Jake in bow tie and dinner jacket and Jim playing only a bodhrán. The disc scrapped into the Top 50 at No 47.

Released in April 1981 the 'Go For It' LP garnered excellent reviews across the music press and provided the band with their fourth consecutive Top 20 album chart placing, peaking at a very respectable No 14. The accompanying 'Go For It' UK tour throughout April and May was another resounding success. The second single culled from the album, 'Silver Lining' b/w 'Safe As House' did less well, reaching only No 68.

In June and July the band embarked on their second US tour, although another short jaunt it included the group's only visit to Canada for a couple of shows.

The latter part of the year brought the news that Jim, uninspired by the newer tracks and impatient to be off to try life in America full-time, had decided to leave the band. Jim's decision briefly prompted Jake to also seriously consider quitting. With things very much undecided the band embarked on a three week French tour over October and November. Jim played his last show with the group on 8 November 1981 at Le Harve. Somewhat surprised by how much he'd enjoyed the dates, Jake felt re-inspired to carry on.

Auditions were held for Jim's replacement, although in reality Jake was determined to have ex-Tom Robinson Band drummer Brian 'Dolphin' Taylor behind the kit. By late November Stiff Little Fingers Mark 3 were in London's Wessex Studios recording a four-track EP.

Captured in front of a tower block in Shepherd's Bush Green, West London. The hi-rise theme fitted with that year's 'Go For It' LP's artwork.

*Above:* Miming 'Just Fade Away' on the BBC's *Top of the Pops*, 2 April 1981.

An original music shop advertisement poster for the 'Just Fade Away' single, March 1981.

Photos from this session featured in the 1981 'Go For It' UK tour programme and various promotional material.

What you see is what you get…
STIFF LITTLE FINGERS

77

**'Go For It' UK Tour 21 April–24 May 1981.** *Support act:* The Wall.

*Above:* An original 'Go For It' tour poster.

Various 'Go For It' UK tour tickets.

*Above* (L to R): Andi Banks, Miko Kurosawa (Japanese music journalist), Ali McMordie, David Stopps' wife, David Stopps (Friars' promoter), Gordon Ogilvie, Jake Burns, Henry Cluney and Jim Reilly, backstage Friars, Aylesbury, 2 May 1981.

Jim Reilly the Europa Hotel, Belfast, April 1981.

Jim and long term girlfriend Siobhan Fahey

Jake, with Gordon Ogilvie behind the speakers, Rainbow, London, 10 May 1981.

Henry, Ali and Jake at the Odeon, Birmingham, 9 May 1981.

Henry at Victoria Hall, Hanley, 30 April 1981.

An original unused ticket for the Newcastle show.

Jim, Jake and Ali. 'Go For It' UK Tour. Venue unknown.

Sean Martin and Spud Murphy 'Go For It' UK tour. Venue Unknown.

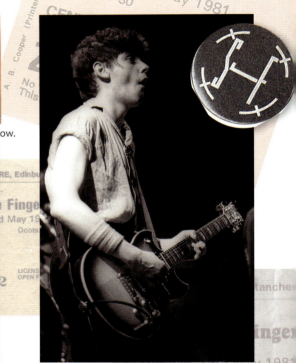

Jake on the 'Go For It' UK tour, City Hall, Newcastle-Upon-Tyne, 18 May 1981.

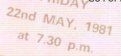

1981 photo session.

*Left:* An alternative shot from the session that provided the front cover photograph for the 'Silver Lining' single.

# North American/Canadian Tour 16 June–10 July 1981.

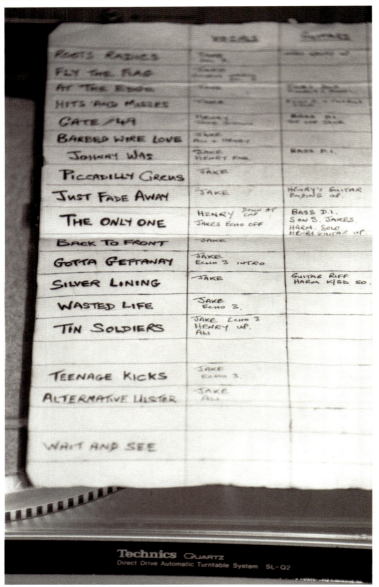

The sound engineer's copy of Stiff Little Fingers' USA/Canadian set list.

*Right:* A letter from Gordon Ogilvie to Canadian photographer Bev Davies.

Jim with a sign that he 'found' attached to a lamppost, 3 July 1981. Photographer Bev Davies recalls: "I arrived in San Francisco to meet up with the band and Jim had the sign backstage with him. It was too good an opportunity to miss!"

*Left:* Jake and Ali, Perkin's Palace, Pasadena, 4 July 1981. In the background, left Wally Grove (SLF's head of security) and right, Paul Roper (SLF's US roadie).

DOA's bassist Randy Rampage and Jim Reilly backstage Old Waldorf, San Francisco, 3 July 1981.

SLF's back line tech Spud Murphy remembers: "That skull and crossed bones t-shirt ended up on a flag pole on a ferry. We were coming back from Sweden and decided it would be a good idea to swap the ship's flag for Jim's t-shirt. The only problem was that when the captain found out what we'd done he was very annoyed and was all set to lock us in the brig. Apparently he could get in real trouble for flying the Jolly Roger at sea! Luckily for us though he was a Clash fan and when he found out who we were he saw the funny side of it."

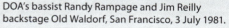

*Top Left:* Henry. *Above:* Jake.
*Left:* Ali backstage.

*All photos:* New Florentine Gardens, Los Angeles, 6 July 1981.

*Right:* Front cover of American SLF Press Pack, 1981.

Jim and the soon to be very famous Siobhan Fahey at home, London, September 1981.

## SPLIT

STIFF LITTLE FINGERS drummer Jim Reilly has quit the band it was announced this week. Or rather, Jim announced that he had fired Stiff Little Fingers and retained the rights to the name Jim Reilly. He's going back to Ireland to look for a new band.

One of the 'sacked members', Gordon Ogilvie, said with tongue firmly in cheek that there were 'bags of hard feelings' over the sacking.

But the remaining members of SLF have managed to get themselves hired by former TRB drummer Dolphin Taylor.

*Sounds* announced Jim's departure from Stiff Little Fingers, 31 October 1981.

**French Tour 20 October–8 November 1981.**

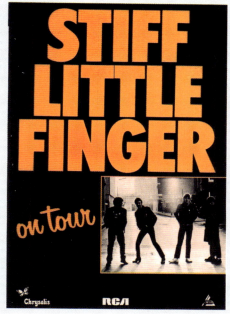

*Left:* 'Stiff Little Finger', an unusable French poster due to the band's name missing the 's' from 'Fingers'.

*Top and above:* Jake and Ali at the last night of the French tour, 1er Salle Francaise, Le Harve, 8 November 1981. The band's farewell banner to Jim, hoisted at the show.

Original poster and tickets from the French tour. Henry: "Whoever designed that poster took a certain advertising licence. We were never an English rock group, nor unfortunately were we ever a No 1 rock group!"

*All photos:* December 1981. This was the first official photo session with Jim Reilly's replacement, ex-TRB sticksman Dolphin Taylor. The session provided the photo for the new look band's first release, the '£1.10 Or Less' EP.

## STIFF LITTLE FINGERS

# 1982
nineteen eighty two

Released in early January the '£1.10 Or Less' EP, so named in an effort to keep the price down, peaked at No 33, thus proving to be the band's second highest charting 7". Another *Top of the Pops* performance, the band's fifth and last, showcased a more serious rock outfit than previous appearances. The short '£3.50 Or Less' UK tour, kept the group busy until the end of January and highlighted the fact that they remained a strong live draw.

April saw the release of 'Talkback' b/w 'Good For Nothing'. The A-side bordered on funk and reiterated how far the band had moved away from their punk rock beginnings. Commercially the disc flopped, being the band's first Chrysalis single not to bother the charts.

Over the summer Stiff Little Fingers were ensconced in London's Jam Studios recording their fourth studio LP. The record would be named 'Now Then' to emphasise the clear definition between the bluster and fury of the band's early sound and their later pop leanings. The LP's release in September was preceded in August by the diamond hard, social commentary of 'Bits Of Kids' b/w 'Stands To Reason'. The only SLF UK single to be released in both 7" and 12" formats, it charted at a lowly No 73.

By late August the band were again back in the USA. Originally booked to play just four shows – two at NYC's Peppermint Lounge and two at Boston's Channel – a fifth performance was added after a large number of young SLF fans had petitioned for the band to play an all-ages show.

Back in Britain, 'Now Then' was released to generally poor reviews and a No 24 chart placing. It was the band's only LP not to enter the Top 20. No US release for the record was planned.

The 'Out Of Our Skulls' UK tour kept the band on the road from the start of October until the middle of November. A number of shows were sparsely attended and the band suddenly found themselves out of tune with many of their fans. Considered an untenable situation by Jake, at the end of a short Scandinavian outing in November he announced to the other band members and Gordon that he was leaving Stiff Little Fingers. After a standalone London show in December, Gordon informed the music press of the split in early 1983.

*Left:* An original advertisement poster for the '£1.10 Or Less' EP.

The band backstage and on stage at the BBC's *Top of the Pops* promoting 'Listen', 27 January 1982.

**'£3.50 Or Less' UK Tour 20–30 January 1982.** *Support act:* **The Flying Padovanis.**

*Above:* Jake, first night of the '£3.50 Or Less' UK tour, Tower Ballroom, Hull, 20 January 1982.

*Right:* Ali and Henry '£3.50 Or Less' UK tour, Colston Hall, Bristol, 26 January 1982.

Various tickets from the tour.

A page from *Smash Hits'* Life Lines, April 1982.

The last night of the '£3.50 Or Less' UK tour,
Friars, Aylesbury, 30 January 1982.

Chrysalis Records promotional shots. All photos taken at a commercial sandpit in Barnet, just outside London. Henry is fairly confident that the shoot took place at the same location that Motorhead's front cover for their classic 'Ace Of Spades' album was taken.

As well as for promotional use, photographs from this session were used for a free poster which could be obtained from the band's fan club with a coupon from the 'Now Then' LP.

What you see is what you get…
STIFF LITTLE FINGERS

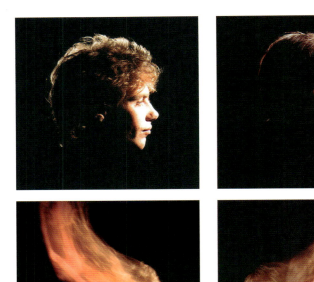

A selection of individual group member photographs from a summer 1982 photo session. The purpose of which was to capture images for the artwork of the 'Bits Of Kids' single, the 'Now Then' LP and for use on various promotional items connected with the upcoming live shows and releases.

SLF manager Gordon Ogilvie at the 'Bits Of Kids'/'Now Then' photo session.

**North American Dates 26–29 August 1982.**

*Above:* Sound check at the (New) Peppermint Lounge, New York City, 27 August 1982.

Henry at sound check.

Back in the USA, for what would prove to be the last time during the group's original time together. Stiff Little Fingers hit the New York streets and the Peppermint Lounge, 27 August 1982.

SLF at sound check.

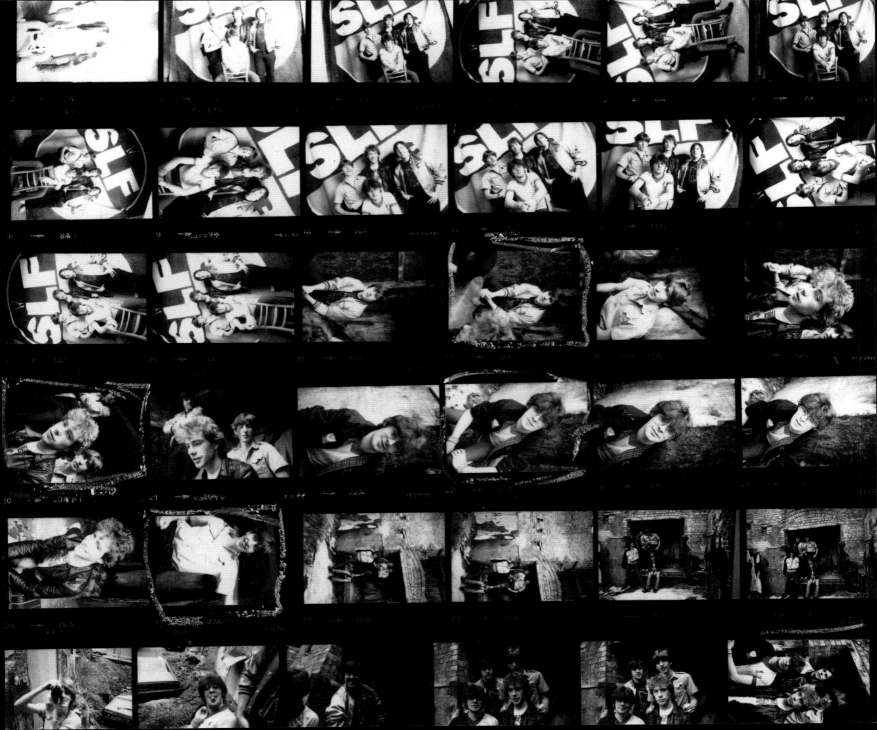

*Melody Maker* – the band's final front page cover for a UK music weekly. The issue also included the free flexi disc pictured below, which coupled snippets of three SLF tracks (all of which subsequently appeared on the 'Now Then' album), with Iggy Pop songs.

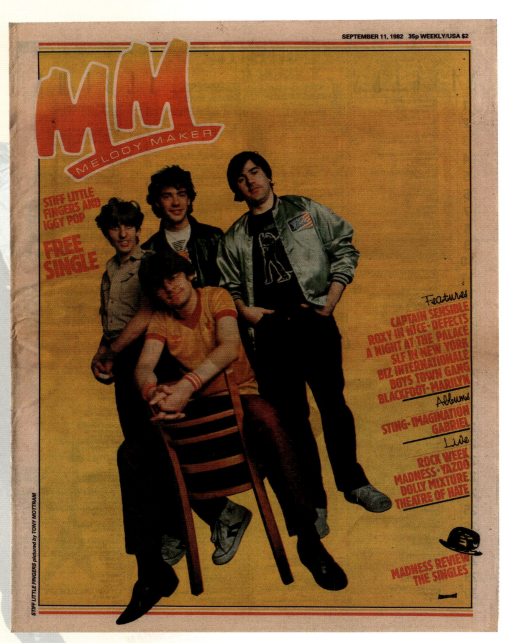

Photographer Tony Mottram: "They stuffed up the front cover. The original has the stage backdrop up behind the band, a nice big SLF logo. Why they had to naffing cut it out I don't know; shit forgot about that. I bet I blew my top at someone over it. I went off to *Sounds* mainly because Garry Bushell poached me and because I wasn't getting enough front covers. The so called *Melody Maker* art dept often mucked up and that could have been the straw that broke the camel's back as far as me leaving was concerned."

*All photos:* BAN Electromusic Rehearsal Studios, London. 23 August 1982.

*All photos:* BAN Electromusic Rehearsal Studios, London. 23 August 1982.

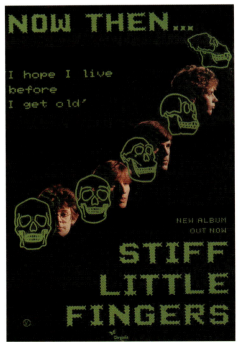
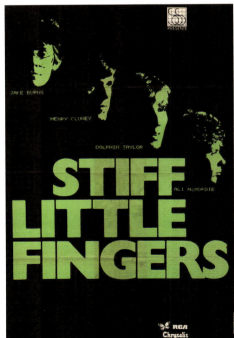

An original 'Now Then' era French poster.

An original 'Now Then' advertisement poster, September 1982.

**'Out Of Our Skulls' UK Tour 3 October–9 November 1982.** *Support act:* **Roddy Radiation And The Tearjerkers.**

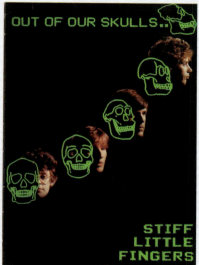

*All photos:* Stiff Little Fingers' signing session, HMV, Newcastle-Upon-Tyne, during the 'Out Of Our Skulls' UK tour, October 1982.

*Above:* Ali with his then wife Christine Southcott in the background wearing his red and black 'Dennis the Menace' style stripped jumper.

*Left:* Tour programme plus various tour tickets.

Tour pass

Jake relaxing in a hotel during the 'Out Of Our Skulls' UK tour October/November 1982.

*Above:* Jake and Ali perform 'The Price of Admission' at the Ulster Hall, Belfast, 8 November 1982. The show was the penultimate date of the 'Out Of Our Skulls' UK tour.

The outing proved to be Stiff Little Fingers' last full scale British tour during their original time together. This Belfast show was their last home town appearance until their triumphant return on the 'Go For It Again' reunion shows in December 1987.

**Scandinavian Dates 16–22 November 1982.**

An original flyer for the Lindblomshallen, Hultsfred, Sweden show, 21 November 1982. The fact that Jim Reilly had left the band the previous year didn't trouble the designer of this particular piece of promotional material.

The following day Jake informed Gordon Ogilvie first and then the other three members of the band that upon their return to the UK he would be leaving the group.

# 1983
nineteen eighty three

Early 1983 saw the end of the band. One final single, 'The Price Of Admission' b/w 'Touch And Go', which had already been scheduled for release before Jake's decision to quit, hit the shops on Friday 4 February. It reached No 102 in the charts. On the same day a double LP of the band's singles called 'All The Best' was also released. It peaked at No 19.

Over the following weekend Stiff Little Fingers played two highly emotional, rammed packed farewell shows. Both took place in traditional SLF strongholds, the first at Newcastle's City Hall, the last one at Glasgow's Apollo. Playing a set list which incorporated tracks from all eras of the band's career the shows brought the first chapter of Stiff Little Fingers' history to a close.

To Anyone who is interested,

I have been asked to write a letter explaining exactly why I am leaving Stiff Little Fingers.

There are a number of reasons and they divide roughly 60% personal and 40% professional. Because 60% of these reasons are personal I'm not going to discuss them here. However, as regards the other 40%, well here goes...

I had decided around about the time Jim left the band that something was wrong within what was left. That was a lack of enthusiasm which luckily returned in part when Dolphin arrived. But it didn't take long for complacency and stubborness to set in again.

There was nothing wrong with the material the band was writing at this period except it lacked ambition. There was no sense of adventure and experiment about it anymore. In other words we had become safe and boring. The things I always hoped we would never become.

So the obvious thing for me to do would have been to leave there and then, i.e. just after the "£1.10 or less" E.P., but being a combination of an optimist and a coward I hoped things would get better.

The "Now Then..." LP was, to my mind, the best album we had made and unfortunately the best I thought we would ever make.

And so I decided after all the tours, (Hello Britain, Ireland, Norway, Sweden and Denmark) I would call it a day.

I fully hope to start writing material for, and with, a new band very shortly and hope you, whoever you are, will bear with both me and the others in whatever they do.

See you soon,
Jake

Jake's open letter to the fan club members, explaining his decision to leave the band.

## Little Fingers stiff

**STIFF LITTLE FINGERS** (above) have announced that they are splitting up after five years of success and as many albums.

Singer **Jake Burns** was the first to go and he comments: "Our last LP 'Now Then' was to my mind the best album we have made. But it is also unfortunately the best I think we will ever make. So I have decided to call it a day".

Burns' decision prompted the decision of drummer **Dolphin Taylor** to "go his own way too".

Burns is currently "writing new material with the intention of getting together another band for recording. But for the moment, no definite details have been settled".

Manager/lyricist **Gordon Ogilvie** was philosophical about the break-up: "Obviously Jake's departure means the end of Stiff Little Fingers as we know it. It could never be the same without him. But the break-up does offer exciting possibilities for the future.

"I hope to continue writing songs with Jake and will back him in what he is going on to do. And if what **Henry, Ali** and I are working on develops as well as we expect, we would hope to produce records through Rigid Digits probably with an official change of name of simply SLF.

"Whatever happens, I am positive the music scene has not heard the last of any of us."

Meanwhile, two shows have been set up at short notice — Newcastle City Hall on February 5 and Glasgow Apollo 6, and a 'bumper double album compilation' of all the band's singles will be rush-released at a special low price.

In January 1983 Stiff Little Fingers let it be known to the wider world that they were to split.

*Sounds*' 'Little Fingers Stiff', *Melody Maker*'s 'Fingers Snapped' and *New Musical Express*' 'Stiffs Stiff Out'; all 15 January 1983 editions.

## Stiffs stiff out

**STIFF LITTLE FINGERS** maintain the current fashion for disbandments, by becoming the first major band in 1983 to break up. The split, just over five years since they were formed in Belfast, is marked by two farewell gigs — at Newcastle City Hall (February 5) and Glasgow Apollo (6).

The end of the line was reached when singer Jake Burns decided to leave the band, so prompting latest drummer Dolphin Taylor also to go his own way. The other two members, Ali McMordie and Henry Cluney, felt that it was impossible for them to continue functioning — "it could never be the same without Jake", they commented.

Explaining his reasons for wanting out, Burns said he considered their last album 'Now Then' to be the best they had made, adding: "Unfortunately, I think it's also the best we would ever make, so I've decided to call it a day". He's now starting to write new material with the intention of getting another band together for recording, though no definite plans have yet been settled.

McMordie and Cluney, together with manager-lyricist Gordon Ogilvie, are going into the studio to experiment with fresh ideas of their own. Taylor may also sit in on their sessions.

As a farewell gesture, a double compilation album of all the band's singles is to be rush released at a special low price. Their production company Rigid Digits has arranged this with their current label Chrysalis, in co-operation with Rough Trade Records who issued their early singles.

## FINGERS SNAPPED

**S**TIFF Little Fingers are splitting up after five years. They're playing two farewell shows at Newcastle City Hall on February 5 and Glasgow Apollo on February 6, and record company Chrysalis are rush-releasing a double album compilation of all their singles to coincide.

The demise of the band was prompted by Jake Burns, who said last week: "Our last album, 'Now Then', was to my mind the best album we have made. But it is also unfortunately the best I think we will ever make. So I have decided to call it a day."

Burns' departure encouraged drummer Dolphin Taylor to do the same. The other two members, Ali McMordie and Henry Cluney, with manager and lyricist Gordon Ogilvie, plan to go into the studio to experiment with fresh ideas of their own.

Taylor, who plans to continue making music with various other artists, will sit in on the sessions.

Says Ogilvie: "Obviously Jake's departure means the end of Stiff Little Fingers as we know it. I hope to continue writing songs with Jake and will back him in what he is going to do.

"And, if what Henry, Ali and I are working on plans out as well as we expect, we would hope to produce records, probably with an official change of name to simply SLF."

Burns is writing new material at the moment and is planning to get another band together for recording.

**Farewell Shows, City Hall, Newcastle 5 February and Apollo, Glasgow 6 February 1983.** *Support act:* **The Alarm.**

An original poster for the last farewell show, plus ticket stubs from the two farewell concerts.

Henry: "On the poster for what was supposed to be the band's last ever show they spelt my name wrong; Harvey Cluney. That seemed to sum the whole thing up really."

### STIFF LITTLE FINGERS
### Glasgow

THE TACKY red and gold glitter of the Glasgow Apollo reflected an affectionate audience and my fears that there might be no one for Stiff Little Fingers to say goodbye to were quickly cancelled. SLF pulled a devoted following out of the woodwork and into what could only be described as a football match.

The place was bristling with unsentimental weekend punks in lurid sweaters, probably wishing they didn't have to go to school tomorrow. Less like a funeral and more like a wake; just as well, as the moments of slush we did have to endure clashed uncomfortably with the honest punk r'n'r.

The band flashed their life before our eyes. An hour and three-quarters condensed the last five years into a staggering 23 numbers — thank God the songs are short or we'd have been there all night — but the audience didn't miss a gesture or forget a word of the desperately performed set. SLF had a wild determination to 'do it right' and their energies were well spent.

Winning my admiration by resisting the urge to simply satisfy the probing of the audience for the late great singles, they paced the set with both old and new and brought home the main points forcefully.

Firstly, that they are still very much on the go with their new single and album and, secondly, they've managed some classically raw songs in the past. And, of course, they are one of the few bands who've managed to break up and still kept both their sense of humour and their dignity.

Zapping back and forth across the years, we were treated to the best of the old: 'Listen', 'Barbed Wire Love', 'Love Of The Common People', the earnest politics of 'Tin Soldiers', plus 'Bits Of Kids' to the brand new but not so powerful 'Falling Down' and the single 'Price Of Admission'.

They scored goals on the audience appreciation chart with 'At The Edge', a brilliantly vitriolic 'Alternative Ulster' and the final encore of 'Wasted Life'.

Overwhelmed by excitement, they poured out their thanks in choked voices, with Oscar-winning sincerity, only succumbing to slush in a flat cover of 'I Love You Love'.

SLF bowed out gracefully with the enthusiasm of a reunion rather than a farewell, and took the bitter edge off their going with a very silly custard pie fight after their last number. They left us with a laugh — the only way to go.

ANDREA MILLER

*Left: Sounds review, written by Jake's girlfriend at the time Andrea Miller.*

**STIFF LITTLE FINGERS: end of the line**

### STIFF LITTLE FINGERS
### Glasgow Apollo

THE five-year reign of Stiff Little Fingers reached a climatic finale with a nuclear blast of a gig at the biggest theatre in Britain.

Jake Burns admitted he was sick at not being able to stage the farewell show in the Fingers' home town of Belfast, but 4,000 fanatical Scots ensured they went out with a bang.

The set, of course, charted the entire SLF history, and when a magnificent "Suspect Device" opened the proceedings, all present knew that for one evening, there was no band on earth that could match them. You name it, they played it. And everything took on a special meaning: "Not Fade Away", "Silver Lining" both *sung*, not growled, proving that over the years even the roughest of voices can improve almost beyond recognition.

"At The Edge", "Wasted Life" and "Barbed Wire Love" got their first airing for ages, and everything they did came out sounding like a classic.

Best of all, though, was the material from the final studio album "Now Then". The Fingers were always a fullblooded rock band, and with songs like "Falling Down" and "Touch And Go" the future of both Burns and Henry Cluney (now leader of a revamped SLF) are assured.

There were still a few tears, however, when they came back for their encore and Cluney let rip with Gary Glitter's "I Love You Love Me Love" with a subtle change of lyric.

But the name of the game was party time and with custard pies from the road crew and two storming closures: "Roots Radicals" and "Fly The Flag", the Fingers made exit stage left to the loudest audience reaction I've ever heard. Good luck SLF — we're all gonna miss you. — NICK KEMP

*Above: Melody Maker review of SLF's final show.*

## Image Credits

All badges and tickets provided by Wayne Connolly, Ian Templeton and Roland Link. Unless stated all other pieces of memorabilia come from the author's collection.

**Eugene Abedari/Rex Features:** 53 all photos
**Janette Beckham:** 23 main
**Adrian Boot/Retna:** 89 all photos
**Brian Cooke/Chrysalis:** 70 and 71 all photos, 87, 94 all photos
**Paul Cox:** 76, 81 inset, 86 all photos
**Kevin Cummins:** 59 black and white photo, 60
**Veuige Dalle/Idols:** 63 all photos
**Bev Davies:** 66 all photos, 67 photo pass, 73 bottom left and top right, 74, 75 all photos, 82 set list and letter, 83 all photos, 84 bottom left
**Siobhan Fahey:** 62 centre right and bottom right colour insets, 79 bottom right
**Brian Faloon:** 19 all photos, 20 bottom right
**Simon Fowler:** 77 top right
**Chris Gabrin/Chrysalis:** front cover, 4, 44 all photos, 46, 47 both photos, 55 all photos, 57 black and white photo
**Alastair Graham:** 14 all photos, 23 inset top, 25 top left, 39 both photos
**Alwyn Greer/Private World Fanzine:** 8, 10 top left
**Ross Halfin:** 67 all photos
**Colin Hall:** 36 all photos except top right
**Sean Hennessy:** 22, 23 inset bottom, 24 all photos, 25 all photos expect top left, 26 and 27 all photos, 79 bottom left and bottom centre
**Mike Layo:** 21
**Mats Lundgren/Chrysalis:** 41 three live photos
**Colin McClelland:** 5 Rigid Digits paper, 8 gig ticket, 13 gig ticket, 14 Rigid Digits Music letter, 21 'Alternative Ulster' sleeve
**Fran McCloskey:** 20 bottom left
**Ali McMordie:** 8 set list

**Lesley Morrall:** 50 top right, 102 all photos except top right
**Tony Mottram:** 97 contact sheet, 99 and 100 all photos
**John Nangle:** 69 Ipswich tour pass, 80 top left, top centre, top right and bottom centre, 85 both photos and tour pass
**Barry Plummer:** 30 all photos, 38 both photos, 42 inset bottom left, 43 and 54 all photos, 56 four colour photos, rear cover
**Ebet Roberts:** 72 all photos, 95, 96 all photos
**Paul Roper:** 73 crew pass, 84 bottom centre
**Tom Sheehan:** 52, 56 four black and white photos
**John Shiels:** 67 MCP tour pass, 68 top left and bottom left, 102 top right
**Cyndy Sproule:** 84 top left and top centre
**Ray Stevenson:** 31, 32 and 33 all photos
**Don Stone:** 40 all photos, 61 two colour photos, 68 top right and bottom right, 69 both photos, 120 background photo.
Courtesy **Ian Templeton:** 104 letter
Courtesy **Jon Templeton:** 103 flyer
**Virginia Turbutt:** 37 all photos, 42 main and inset bottom right, 61 black and white photo
**Mick Warrender:** 62 main and top two black and white insets
**Chris Walter/Retna:** 73 top left and bottom right
**Rick Walton:** 15, 16, 17 and 18 all photos, 80 bottom right, 101 all photos
**Jane Williams:** 92 main
**Pip Williams:** 29 backstage pass, 66 set list
**Sarah Woods:** 49 all photos, 50 all photos except top right, 57 two colour photos, 62 bottom left two colour insets
**Brian Young:** 12 gig poster
**Unknown Photographers:** 10 main, 12, 20 top left, 34 all photos, 36 top right, 41 all photos from 'Straw Dogs' studio session, 59 colour photos, 77 colour photos, 79 top right, 80 bottom left, 81 main, 88, 90 both photos, 92 inset, 93 all photos

# Rare Vinyl Guide

## Singles

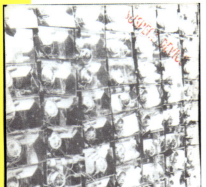

*Original*

*One of two variants*

### Suspect Device

There's only one place to begin when assessing collectable SLF vinyl, and that's at the start, the very start, with 'Suspect Device'.

Manufactured by Dublin based company, Cardel (or possibly Carlton Productions – see below), the first copies saw light of day on 17 March 1978. Financed by Gordon Ogilvie and released on the now ubiquitous Rigid Digits Label, the initial batch of 500 are unique. Carrying the legendary SRD-1 catalogue number this first run are the 'real deal'.

How do you know if you've got one? Easy. The labels are red, SRD-1 is on the right-hand side and underneath the Rigid Digits crest is written 'Records'.

More importantly, certainly from a value point of view, the cover is also distinct. Later copies came housed in well-produced and professionally printed sleeves. The first 500, however, came in photocopied sleeves. They are easily identified because 'Suspect Device' appears in the top right hand corner – it's in the top left on all subsequent versions. And the rear cover shot of the band is clearly a black and white photocopy.

Some copies have a handwritten number '2' in black ink on the B-side. Supposedly put on by the band during the well documented 'folding and gluing' session in Ogilvie's flat. When recently quizzed, Brian Faloon's only recollection was: "that is very possible due to extreme boredom. I believe we wrote some things on labels and in the sleeves, but I couldn't say with absolute certainty." Presumably they weren't keen on the clearly visible A and B-side references!

In recent times these original versions have changed hands on eBay for up to £200. A staggering amount of money bearing in mind Ogilvie originally bankrolled the band £500 for the whole first consignment.

There are two variants of this first version in circulation. Possibly second and third smaller run pressings, the discs came without sleeves and are almost exactly the same as the originals. Both have slight but distinct variations in the typesetting.

The first differs in that the 'M' of 'Music' has clearly shifted to the left, and sits under the first 'i' of 'Rigid'. On the first pressing the 'M' is clearly below the 'g' of 'Rigid'. The RIGID DIGITS arc is also spaced noticeably further from the copyright statement on the perimeter of the label. On the other the RIGID DIGITS arc is again clearly spaced differently whereby the lettering is equidistant between the copyright message and the word RECORDS. The 'I' of RIGID is also aligned differently with the copyright wording on the label edge.

To the best of my knowledge, there were five further pressings released independently by the band. All had professional machine cut sleeves manufactured by Delgar with 'Suspect Device' written in red in the top left-hand corner. On the back the picture has been upgraded from photocopy to proper black and white image.

The exact order of release is unknown, but it's likely the second large batch were those with the distinctive yellow labels. Other than being yellow, these are identical to the un-sleeved second run.

'Suspect Device' – SRD-1 various pressings
Far left: White label
Centre left: 'Original Recording Belfast'
Left: 'Side 1' label
Below: Miss-press label

It's a fair bet that the white/cream batch followed. For these the typesetting has been overhauled, the 'Records' reference has been dropped and 'Rigid Digits Music' has moved to the left hand side of the label. A few copies have true 'white' labels (rather than the dirty off-white appearance on most), but I've yet to see a copy with two perfect white faces.

Both the yellow and white/cream versions are reasonably easy to track down. And depending on condition and the existence of an accompanying sleeve you can expect to pay anything up to £40 a copy.

The remaining three versions all have red labels. The most common of the three and probably the largest individual pressing, has SRD-1 moved to the left of the disc, whilst the Side A and 45 RPM references are now on the right. Invariably if you see a red label 'Suspect Device' on eBay it will be this one. A nice copy complete with smart sleeve will set you back about £20.

Somewhat rarer and consequently more expensive should you track one down, is the version with the unique 'Original Recording Belfast, 1978' running along the foot of the label. These will set you back roughly £30.

The final version is again unique in that it's the only issue to make reference to 'SIDE 1' as opposed to 'SIDE A'. This is extremely rare and, assuming the seller knows what they've got, would probably set you back anything up to £75.

Contrary to prevailing rumour there never was a green labelled version.

**Miss-Press**
There is an incredibly rare miss-press of the standard red label version without the RIGID DIGITS arc on Side A. Extremely collectable should a copy ever come up you would likely be looking to pay upwards of £200.

**Test Pressing**
Test pressings with blank 'dirty' red labels were produced. I've no idea how many were circulated and the cost to acquire one would, I imagine, be upwards of £250.

**Matrix Numbers**
All variations carry the same matrix numbers etched into the wax. Side A shows: SRD - 1 - A - 1 with Side B showing: SRD - 1 - B - 1. In addition both faces have the interlinked letters T & B.

**Rear Sleeve Picture**
Forgetting the paper sleeve original, there are three different variants of the group shot used on the rear cover. One is high definition, one is dark with little detail and the third is somewhere between the two. The best way to tell the difference is by studying the detail on Burns' leather jacket. On the high definition version you can see all the creases whereas the dark version is a very basic photograph with nearly all the definition removed.

It is unclear which version goes with which batch issue, but I'd guess that the high definition version came with the most common red label run.

**Suspect Device Pressing Plant**
There never was a record pressing plant in Northern Ireland, as such labels and bands had to look to Dublin.

# HEY, PUNKS – THAT'S ME ON YOUR RECORD COVER!

*John finds his face on the latest rock single*

The first pressing plant in the Republic was opened in Ferrybank, County Waterford and was owned by EMI.

There was, as far as I know, only one other and that was Carlton Productions run by Robbie McGrattan. Based on JFK Industrial Estate in Dublin 12 it was on Dublin's southside.

As I understand it Carlton were happy to press as little as 200 copies of any given disc. This would sit nicely with Ogilvie's requirements and the various subsequent re-pressings, but somewhere along the line the name Cardel seems to have taken hold. Whichever is correct remains unclear.

## Everything Else

From here on in you'll be glad to know it gets a lot simpler. Taking each single release in order, I'm aware of the following rarities/oddities, none of which came with covers unless specified:

## Alternative Ulster

The first Rough Trade run was erroneously printed up with 78 RPM shown as the A-side and 'Alternative Ulster' on the flip. These change hands for circa £30.

There are also a very few copies with 78 RPM B-side labels on both disc faces. Due to their scarcity, these would probably command a price of circa £70, possibly more.

Copies with a standard 'Alternative Ulster' A-side label and a blank white label on the flip have been seen and will attract interest at circa £100.

Best and rarest of all, however, are the few surviving copies with different 'Alternative Ulster' labels on either side. One reading 'A Side' and the reverse 'B Side'. Expect to pay £125+.

## Suspect Device

I'm not aware of any non-standard versions of the Rough Trade release although there are white label test pressings. Extremely rare, one could easily set you back £175+.

'Alternative Ulster' – Miss-press

I've also seen a version with a white label A-side and a standard Wasted Life label on the flip. Again, extremely rare.

As with the Rigid Digits releases the rear sleeve picture exists in at least two forms. One high definition, the other much darker and consequently lacking in detail.

## Gotta Gettaway

The only 'Gotta Gettaway' variant I know of is a mis-press with Bloody Sunday B-side labels on both faces. Mega rare and valued at £150+.

There is, of course, the uniquely packaged French 12" on Celluloid Records. Readily available on import and still quite easy to come by. You should be able to pick up a decent copy with standard black labels for around £10.

Harder to find are those with the attractive blue and white labels. These may set you back nearer £25.

The covers also differ slightly. All the red text on the black label sleeve has a yellow tint. Presumably a minor printing error? By contrast, the cover housing the blue and white label copies is sharply defined. I suspect the latter were the originals.

## Rough Trade 7" Labelling

From the amount of miss-pressed disc labelling that is known to exist it's clear that Rough Trade had a few production line 'issues'. On this basis I'm sure other undocumented permutations also exist and I'd be interested to hear from anyone who can provide additional information.

*German label*

*'Straw Dogs' – German cover*

## Straw Dogs

I've never seen a promo of this, the first single on Chrysalis, but there are a number of foreign pressings available.

All with their own unique labels, there are copies from Ireland, Germany (this comes with a cover similar to its UK counterpart, but with an added reference number in the top left hand corner and some label information in German on the rear bottom left) and Australia. All have 'You Can't Say Crap On The Radio' as the B–side.

The German copy is relatively easy to find (£15), the Australian less so (expect to pay circa £25). The Irish version is increasingly difficult to track down and could cost as much as £50.

There were a number of miss-pressed copies that escaped quality control at the pressing plant and, although stamped, the B–sides are not coloured blue and remain black. These are pretty scarce and can fetch up to £25.

## At The Edge

Again, no UK promo to my knowledge, but six alternate discs can be found.

The most interesting is the Dutch version. Complete with a unique cover it has 'Straw Dogs' on the B–side. A decent copy will set you back up to £40.

Its French counterpart has silver labels and will probably cost around £10. There's also a French promo version that comes without a cover and has 'Gotta Gettaway' on the flip side. If you can find one, you will again have to fork out around £40, maybe more.

In addition, there are Irish, Australian and New Zealand pressings to collect. Expect to pay about £35 for the Irish copy and between £25 and £30 for the Australian and Kiwi versions.

*'At The Edge' – Dutch pressing cover and labels*

*Front*

*Rear*

*'At The Edge' – New Zealand pressing*

111

*'Nobody's Hero' – Italian 7"*

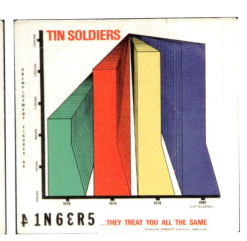

*'Nobody's Hero' – Promo disc*

### Nobody's Hero

The first Chrysalis single to come in promo form, the disc is clearly stamped 'For Promotional Use Only'. Increasingly scarce, expect to pay in the order of £35 to secure a copy.

The disc contains an edited version of the song lasting three minutes and twelve seconds. The standard version runs for four minutes and twelve seconds.

Similar to 'At The Edge' there is also a French pressed version with silver labels. Expect to pay £10.

'Nobody's Hero' was Fingers' only Italian 7" pressing. It comes with a sleeve mirroring that of the UK release, but has its own unique catalogue number (6198 365) shown on the front. The reference to both tracks being taken from 'Nobody's Heroes' has been removed from the bottom left hand side and there's a 'Made in Italy' reference on the rear.

It's also printed on paper as opposed to the stiff card used for the UK sleeve. Decent copies are hard to come by and will set you back £30+.

There is also an elusive Irish pressing. Interestingly the disc features the three minute and twelve second edited version featured on the UK promo rather than the full length track. Definitely the rarest of the Irish releases it's likely to cost circa £50.

### Back To Front

Again, no UK promo that I'm aware of.

Like 'Straw Dogs', there were a handful of miss-pressed copies with stamped, but blank, black B–sides. These are exceptionally rare and can fetch up to £60.

Known foreign pressings emanate from Germany and Ireland.

The defining detail on the German version is that 'Back To Front' is misspelt on the label as 'Back To Frent'. The cover is again the same as the UK version, but it carries additional detail regarding catalogue numbers.

*'Back To Front' – German pressing*

The German copy is quite common and should cost about £15. The Irish version less so and consequently you'll pay circa £35, possibly more.

### Just Fade Away

Chrysalis issued a nice two-track promo to promote 'Just Fade Away'. Catalogued as SLFDJ 1, the disc plays at 45 RPM and has blue and white two-tone labels. The single track B-side carries 'Go For It'. (The standard release

*'Nobody's Hero' – Irish pressing*

*'Just Fade Away'* – Promo

*'Just Fade Away'* – Swedish pressing (top centre and above)

plays at 33⅓ RPM and has 'Go For It' and 'Doesn't Make It Alright' on the flip side.) Frequently advertised on the likes of eBay, a copy will cost you round about £15.

Four foreign pressings also exist. Australian and New Zealand copies are scarce and will cost between £20 and £30.

The other two are even harder to find. The first, the band's only Scandinavian single release, comes from Sweden and will cost you upwards of £40. The second, an Irish release, will again set you back £40 or more.

## Silver Lining

Another of the mysterious 'no UK promo' singles. Known variations come from Ireland and Australia.

The Irish version will cost up to £35, the Australian possibly a little more.

## Listen

The lack of a 'Silver Lining' promo is all the more peculiar when you consider, in a similar vein to 'Just Fade Away', Chrysalis produced a distinctive promo copy for 'Listen'. Carrying the unique catalogue number CHSDJ 2580 and again with the distinctive blue and white two-tone labels, the disc has differing versions of 'Listen' on both sides. Side A is a three minutes fifty radio edit, whilst the full four minute seventeen second version is on the flip. Appearing reasonably regularly on eBay, a nice copy can probably be yours for around £20.

There is also a silver labelled two track (abridged 'Listen' on the A, 'Two Guitars Clash' on the B) 'juke-box' version. It also carries the CHSDJ 2580 catalogue number and will again cost up to £20.

An Irish version exists and will cost round about £30. (Interestingly 'Listen' was the only SLF single to make the Irish charts. It featured for two weeks only and reached number 24.)

As with most SLF singles there was also an Australian release. 7" promo copies of the record carrying the Chrysalis styled DJ-152 cataloguing exist and interestingly carry identical versions of 'Listen' on both sides. Expect to pay £40 plus for one of these.

However, the standard Australian release was issued as a 12". The front cover uses the band photograph shown in the top right hand corner of the UK 7" release sleeve with each individual's full name detailed under STIFF LITTLE FINGERS. The rear carries adverts for the band's various studio albums to date. Incredibly scarce, if you can find a copy it could cost you upwards of £40.

*'Silver Lining'* – Irish pressing

*'Listen'* – Promo (above) and juke-box issue (left)

113

'Listen' – Australian 7" promo (left)

'Listen' – Australian 12" cover and rear (right)

### Talkback

Inexplicably and frustratingly there is no known UK promo. Maybe only alternate releases were afforded the extra expense of a promotional copy?

Equally peculiar is the fact that for reasons unknown, 'Talkback' was the only SLF single to have a Spanish release. The sleeve is essentially the same as the UK version, but at the foot of the rear there is some additional company and copyright detail together with reference in Spanish to what looks like the local distribution company (I don't speak Spanish!). Expect to pay about £15.

As always, the Australians and Irish issued their own unique versions and the costs of acquiring will be roughly in line with those detailed previously.

### Bits Of Kids

By the time of SLF's penultimate 7" release it appears the Australians had unfortunately lost interest, as there is no known antipodean version.

Chrysalis did issue a UK blue and white labelled two-tone promo though, with the unique reference of CHS 2637DJ. It carries the same versions of 'Bits of Kids' and 'Stands To Reason' that appeared on the single proper. Arguably the rarest of the (known) UK promos, you may have to pay up to £60 to secure a copy.

A silver labelled French copy was also made and as with the other French releases will cost you approximately £10 to secure.

There is an Irish version, but they are incredibly scarce. Interestingly, for reasons unknown, the 'Made in Ireland' reference has been dropped from both labels. Expect to pay up to £50.

'Talk Back' – Spanish pressing and rear cover

'Bits of Kids' – Promo

## The Price Of Admission

In line with my (possibly ridiculous) theory there is again no known UK Chrysalis promo. And it appears no one else, not even the faithful Irish arm of Chrysalis, were prepared to issue the band's final single as there are no known foreign variations out there.

## Irish Pressings

All the Irish Chrysalis releases were produced in Dublin (as incidentally were discs for Good Vibrations, IT and Rip Off Records) specifically for sale in Ireland. Numbers were limited and an initial pressing of 500 was standard.

In Northern Ireland the shops carried the UK pressings as the norm, albeit many of the Irish issued discs were in circulation.

Over recent years these singles have become increasingly popular with American and Japanese collectors and as a result have become scarce and, as detailed, expensive.

## Australian and New Zealand Pressings

All the Australian and New Zealand releases were issued on Chrysalis via Festival Records.

For reasons unknown, with the exception of the 12" 'Listen', none were issued with picture sleeves.

I have it on good authority that 'Nobody's Hero', 'Back To Front', 'Bits Of Kids' and 'The Price Of Admission' were never afforded an Australian release.

## Juke-Box Singles

There are various discs knocking around adapted to play on 7" juke-box machines, but save for the enlarged centre hole they are exactly the same as the standard issue records. Cut with a special tool they are effectively just vandalized discs!

## Acetates

An acetate disc is one made for quality control prior to the cutting of the master disc from which retail copies of the record will be pressed. It is an aluminium disc coated with a fine film of nitro-cellulose lacquer and contains no actual 'acetate'.

It is almost always single-sided (the other side is blank and shiny, with no grooves and no label), heavier and usually more rigid than vinyl. Its purpose is to serve as a reference disc to allow the quality of the recording process to be checked. If the engineer makes any adjustments to the sound the acetate allows the producer to approve these changes. The lacquer coating on the disc is very soft and the sound quality will deteriorate the more you play it, diminishing the high frequencies and increasing the surface noise.

Essentially, if you have an 'acetate', you have a disc that was cut for the producer, engineer and artist to listen to.

Over the years I've amassed the grand total of three SLF acetates. Or put another way, that's roughly one for every ten years of searching! They are undoubtedly the serious record collector's 'holy grail'.

The ones I've been lucky enough to source are 'Back To Front', 'Just Fade Away' and 'The Price Of Admission'. 'Back To Front' and 'Just Fade Away' were both cut at Trident Recording Studios in Wardour Street, London and, unusually, both are double-sided. 'The Price Of Admission' disc was cut at The Master Room in West London and is single-sided.

'Back To Front' – Acetate

'Just Fade Away' – Acetate

'The Price Of Admission' – Acetate

## Albums

There are a myriad of foreign pressed Stiff Little Fingers albums and unfortunately there just isn't space here to go through them all. However, there are a few nice items worthy of special mention:

### Christmas Album

The only bootleg album to surface during the band's original incarnation, the 'Christmas Album' features a particularly exuberant recording of a show at the Music Palais, Stockholm, Sweden on 5 December 1979. Both labels are white and the A-side is simply stamped in purple ink.

The album comes with a wonderful black and white wraparound photocopied sleeve. The front cover features a shot of the band from the night and the wraparound flap gives details of the tracks together with passport size mug shots of the four band members.

Reportedly limited to 300 discs sale copies, hardly ever surface. If they do it's likely you'll need to pay in excess of £100 to add it to your collection.

'The Christmas Album' – Bootleg

### 'Nobody's Heroes' Promo Album and Cover Test Art

Purchased from a certain R Link at a clandestine meeting just off the M5, it's fair to say this ultra-rare item takes pride of place in my collection. The disc is unremarkable, the standard 'Heroes' promo with white labels and a large 1 and 2 printed on the respective labels. However, it's the artwork that makes this particular gem unique.

As most readers will know, in a mischievous move the standard rear album artwork depicted a genuine rebuttal letter the band had received from Chrysalis two years previously. However, artistic freedom aside, there was only so far these cheeky young punks could push their new benefactors, and to avoid embarrassment, the visionary author had his name and signature conveniently airbrushed.

The original album proofs, however, were not so deferential. As well as showing the track listing in strictly alphabetical order, it's clear that venerable A&R supremo Chris Briggs wrote the infamous letter and was the butt of this particular joke.

The joke did backfire somewhat, because Gordon Ogilvie's Belfast address was left on the published sleeve. Not surprisingly, the new incumbents (Ogilvie had moved on) were subsequently inundated with unwanted demo tapes and correspondence. So much in fact that 1981's 'Go For It' included an appeal to fans to stop writing!

Being the fall guy didn't adversely affect Briggs' music business career. A big wig at EMI, he's brought the world numerous acts and had the (dubious?) honour of guiding Robbie Williams' meteoric rise.

There have been at least two subsequent re-issues of the album both no doubt now collectible in their own right, however, from a collector's viewpoint neither can touch the original.

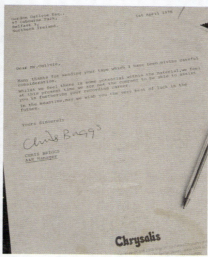

'Nobody's Heroes' – Cover test art with Chris Briggs signature

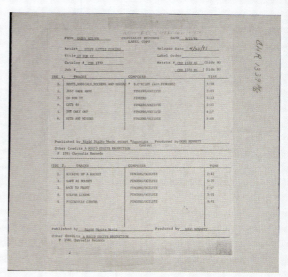

'Go For It' – US test pressing sleeve

'Go For It' – US test pressing label (above) and Press Pack (left)

## US 'Go For It' Test Pressing and Press Pack

The album itself is of note because, unlike its UK equivalent, the US version includes an extra track, 'Back To Front'.

Produced in Santa Maria, the Columbia Record Productions test press disc is unbelievably rare. It carries white labels stamped with black ink informing the reader that: "This is a test pressing intended for use in determining the technical quality of the recording only. It is not intended for sale or distribution outside of this company."

Protected in a plain white card sleeve, a data sheet is cellotaped to the front confirming track detail, release dates and the individual dealing with the promotion. In this case a certain Kathy Nelson.

The package is completed by the official Chrysalis Records 'Go For It' press pack. Housed in a tailor made yellow and blue card jacket depicting the boy with the outstretched hand from the album cover art, it contains a two page biography, a glossy black and white band photograph and contact details for Chrysalis in Los Angeles and New York.

To buy the complete kit would, I imagine, cost the best part of £100, possibly more.

*'Go For It' – Spanish album*

*'Nobody's Heroes' – Japanese album*

## Spanish 'Go For It'

Unique in that the front cover features the motif from the 'Talkback' single. No inner sleeve, but highly prized and very hard to find. If you are offered one expect to fork out something in the region of £75, maybe more.

## Japanese Albums

I wanted to include reference to these albums purely because they are genuinely lovely items to behold.

To the best of my knowledge there isn't an 'Inflammable Material' or a 'Now Then'. But Chrysalis via Toshiba-EMI did produce unique versions of 'Nobody's Heroes', 'Go For It' and 'Hanx'.

Each disc is completed by the ubiquitous 'Obi-strip'. Or the fifth-of-a-cover width paper sleeve that provides the browser the necessary album detail in Japanese. (Or at least that's what I've always assumed they say.)

### 'Nobody's Heroes'

Produced in a high quality card sleeve, the cover detail is as per the front and rear UK album version. However, it is distinct in that there is a Japanese inscription at the bottom of the rear cover and a 'made in Japan' motif.

The insert is a double-sided replica of the UK inner sleeve on yellow paper with additional Japanese text on the reverse.

The record labels are variants on the standard Chrysalis blue and white two-tone and contain no Japanese hieroglyphics.

The obi-strip is predominantly white and red and appears to detail the song titles as well as other information.

### 'Hanx'

Again in a glossy, sturdy card sleeve the format is as per the UK version with the addition of the Japanese writing and 'made in Japan' on the centre bottom of the reverse.

Unlike its UK counterpart it comes with a double-sided white paper inner replicating the song titles and lyrics. They're in Japanese on the front side and English on the flip. Although someone has no doubt done their level best, the translations are brilliantly inaccurate. I especially like the first line of verse three in Wait and See, 'We were charted, a pillow in every lane'. Or perhaps you prefer, 'Armies for the free, and silly whores' lifted direct from Wasted Life.

The labels are blue and white two-tone as per 'Nobody's Heroes'.

The 'Hanx' obi is a colourful black-based affair with an Irish tri-colour at the top. The back appears to promote 'Nobody's Heroes' and a Rory Gallagher album.

*Sleeve cover*

*Sleeve reverse*

*Insert front*

*Left and above: 'Hanx' – Japanese album sleeve*

*Below and bottom: 'Go For It' – Japanese album sleeve*

**'Go For It'**

As above, the sleeve is of well-made card and replicates its UK cousin with the added Japanese text situate centre bottom rear.

Again, the inner is a double-sided sheet. The front carries the familiar Lots Road, Chelsea street shot overwritten in Japanese with the album track listing detail (in English and Japanese) and all the lyrics in Japanese. The rear reproduces the UK inner text in white on black (the UK version being red on black).

The labels are standard blue and white, but mine also has a neat and delicate Japanese stamp on side one. (Possibly a radio station copy or similar?)

The front of the obi has a black background with attractive blue and white writing. The rear is white and carries adverts for 'Heroes' and 'Hanx'.

*'Go For It' – Japanese album*

### Promotional Copies

Each of the three albums was also produced in promo format. The packaging is the same (including obi), but the discs carry distinct white labels with black writing. The bulk is English, but there is also a little Japanese.

### Cost

Beware, these discs can be expensive, but play your cards right and you shouldn't have to pay more than £45 a piece (maybe up to £65 for the promos). On the plus side, being a meticulous lot the Japanese look after things and invariably whenever you buy a copy, especially direct from the source country, it's likely to be in immaculate condition.

However, before you part with your cash make sure the 'Obi-strip' is present and intact. If it's not, your record is incomplete and the price ought to reflect as much.

## BBC Transcription Discs

There are a number of 12" BBC transcription discs featuring Stiff Little Fingers.

Transcription Services was a commercial arm of the BBC (it is now called Radio International) that supplied BBC programming to radio stations around the globe. They would monitor the output of the BBC stations and, in some instances, produce their own programming for sale overseas. *Top of the Pops* was a hybrid of the two, their own series using music from various BBC shows like Saturday Club, Top Gear, or Radio 1 sessions alongside commercial discs.

Offered on vinyl and reel-to-reel tape, only limited numbers were ever produced, and the normal agreements for use were for a set number of broadcasts within a short period (normally a couple of years, but dependent on the type of programming), with the discs either returned to the BBC or, more often, 'destroyed'. Although I am sure some were smashed, many found their way out of the 'back doors' of radio stations and a trade built up amongst collectors, although not in the UK as publications like Record Collector would not carry adverts for them due to them not being officially available. This is likely because they were for export only and, as such, duty was never paid on them in the UK.

The discs are rarely traded and extraordinarily hard to find. They tend to feature singles rather than album tracks and I'm aware of copies carrying 'At The Edge', 'Nobody's Hero', 'Back to Front', 'Just Fade Away', 'Silver Lining' and 'Listen'. Complete versions include a cue sheet, chart rundown detail and an information sheet.

If you're offered one snap it up, but complete copies may set you back up to £100 a piece.

### Autographs

The band always made themselves available to sign items and consequently there is a lot of signed material around. Regardless, if you have the correct set of signatures on a cover and/or disc the value increases considerably.

Of the band members Brian Faloon's signature is undoubtedly the rarest. Items signed by Gordon Ogilvie and Colin McClelland would also fetch a premium price.

### Record Values

All the values I've used are, of course, subjective and made on the assumption the disc and, where relevant, cover are mint condition or thereabouts. Consequently they can only be used as a best guide and if you're lucky you'll pay far less and hopefully be totally satisfied.

---

My contribution to this book has been a labour of love, but without help it would be considerably less impressive. So my heartfelt thanks and gratitude go to:

Neil Phillips for uncomplainingly photographing my whole collection and, against the odds, maintaining a facade of genuine interest – what a professional, cheers mate!

Jake Templeton, Pete Noone and Mac Templeton for additional photography.

Steve Arnold for supplying the authoritative BBC transcription disc information.

Ant Davie, Yair Goodfellow, Jeff Skinner, Mick Warrender, Sarah and Len Woods, Anna Link, The Ainsleys, Gary Thompson, Simon Barraclough and The Mockfords for being good people.

Malcolm Johnston at Colourpoint for taking us on and singlehandedly seeing the job through regardless of the endless alterations, updates and revisions.

My beautiful boys, Jake and Louis, and their beautiful mum, Caroline, for being healthily disinterested in the whole escapade. Great for keeping my feet firmly on the ground – I love you all beyond words.

Brother Jon for pitching in and parents, Janet and Mac, for fronting my ebay skirmishes and surreptitiously delivering illicit packages when the home coast is clear.

Bristol Rovers for being reassuringly hopeless, but still we live in hope of a new stadium and glory days ahead!

And, of course, Ro, thanks for indulging me and allowing me to yet again ride your coattails.

Ian Templeton, May 2014